Praise for

JACKIE'S GIRL

"McKeon's delightful memories have been tucked away for fifty years, and thankfully, she has brought them out to share the enchanting magic of Camelot with us all."

—*Kirkus Reviews*

"Celebrity watchers who covet an insider's role will find McKeon's frank yet benevolent memoir to be both a sobering reality check and an engaging foray into the ever-fascinating world of the Kennedy dynasty."

—*Booklist*

"Recommended for general readers, especially those interested in the Kennedy administration and its 'Camelot' era."

—*Library Journal*

"A rare and engrossing look at the private life of one of the most famous women of the twentieth century, *Jackie's Girl* is also a moving personal story of a young woman finding her identity and footing in a new country, along with the help of the most elegant woman in America."

—Bustle.com

". . . a fascinating account of a young, uneducated woman who came of age and matured in a most extraordinary environment."

—Bookreporter.com

JACKIE'S GIRL

My Life with the Kennedy Family

Kathy McKeon

Gallery Books

New York   London   Toronto   Sydney   New Delhi

G

Gallery Books
An Imprint of Simon & Schuster, Inc.
1230 Avenue of the Americas
New York, NY 10020

First Gallery Books trade paperback edition March 2018

GALLERY BOOKS and colophon are registered trademarks of Simon & Schuster, Inc.

For information about special discounts for bulk purchases,
please contact Simon & Schuster Special Sales at 1-866-506-1949
or business@simonandschuster.com.

The Simon & Schuster Speakers Bureau can bring authors to your live event. For more
information or to book an event, contact the Simon & Schuster Speakers Bureau
at 1-866-248-3049 or visit our website at www.simonspeakers.com.

Interior design by Davina Mock-Maniscalco

Manufactured in the United States of America

10   9   8   7   6   5   4   3   2

Library of Congress Cataloging-in-Publication Data
McKeon, Kathy, author. Jackie's girl : my life with the Kennedy family / Kathy McKeon.
New York : Gallery Books, 2017. | Description based on print version record and CIP data
    provided by publisher.
LCCN 2017003981 (print) | LCCN 2017016548 (ebook)
LCSH: McKeon, Kathy. | Onassis, Jacqueline Kennedy, 1929–94—Friends and associates.
    | Women household employees—United States—Biography. | Irish American women—
    United States—Biography. | Household employees—United States—Biography. | Kennedy
family. Classification: LCC CT275.O552 (ebook) | LCC CT275.O552 M35 2017 (print)
    | DDC 973.922092 [B] —dc23
LC record available at https://lccn.loc.gov/2017003981

ISBN 978-1-5011-5894-0
ISBN 978-1-5011-5895-7 (pbk)
ISBN 978-1-5011-5896-4 (ebook)

To Jackie—

*Your extraordinary courage and strength were an inspiration for me,
and strongly influenced the proud mother and grandmother that
I am today. Thank you for allowing me into your family.*

To John and Caroline—

*I believe that individuals come in and out of our lives for a reason,
and that we need to slow down long enough to reflect
on how they may have influenced who we are today. It's hard
to put into words exactly how your mother influenced me . . .
but I have tried to capture it here in my memories of her
and of the both of you. Thank you for allowing me
to share these memories with others.*

*"If you produce one book, you will have done
something wonderful in your life."*
—Jackie Onassis

Where Were You When It Happened?

In 1964, the shock of President Kennedy's assassination was still fresh, and the question felt more urgent than casual, popping up the way it did at bus stops and lunch counters, on church steps and park benches, within moments of meeting someone for the first time. It was as if everyone thought that collectively reliving that last moment of innocence might somehow help us recapture what was lost forever. That question would linger for five years, then ten, then fifty. . . .

But in 1964, people were already beginning to reframe their lives around it.

At nineteen, I was still too naive, though, too foreign, to grasp its significance. My worldview back then was no bigger than the servants' quarters of the wealthy Manhattan households where I worked—making beds, polishing crystal, and caring for the well-groomed children of posh society women. I was really no more than a child myself when Jacqueline Kennedy came into my life and made me part of hers.

I was in Caroline's room one afternoon soon after I was hired when the question was directed at me. I froze for a panicked moment. No one had told me what to say, if there were rules I was to follow, or an answer I was meant to give. If the slain president's seven-year-old daughter all of a sudden wanted to know: "Where were you when it happened, Kath?"

Caroline, more than anyone, deserved an answer—of that much I was certain. I would have to trust that even at such a tender age, she had already learned in the months since her father's murder what reminders of him might ease her heartache. After all, it was she who had broached the delicate subject. She had been showing me some of her favorite storybooks and toys when she paused and looked up at me.

"Did you know my father was president of the United States, and that he got shot?"

"Yes, I did know," I answered carefully. "And I'm so sorry that happened, Caroline."

The words felt too thin to hold the weight of the moment, but Caroline seemed happy, not sad, to be talking about him.

"Were you here or back in Ireland?"

I told her I had been back home, in a wee village called Inniskeen, where I lived on a small farm with my parents and seven brothers and sisters. Caroline pressed me to go on.

"The people in Ireland must be very sad, because my daddy was Irish, and very popular and people loved him," she said. I was surprised that she seemed to know about her father's deep bond with my homeland, and I could tell she was hungry to hear more about it firsthand.

"You're right," I said. "We were all very sad. Every family had a picture of your father hanging up in their house, right next to the pope's. My mother kept ours right there in the kitchen."

"Where were you when it happened, Kath?"

Keeping my voice steady and calm, I told her my story.

"There was a dance in the village every Friday," I began. "My older sister, Briege, and I would always go with our friends." We would spend hours getting ready, putting together our outfits and curling our hair using strips of clean rag. First we'd tie a length of cloth into a loose circle, then take a section of damp hair and wrap it around the circle before tying the two ends of the rag together tight. By the time our hair dried and we untied our rag curlers, we'd have ringlets to style into a bouncy sock-hop ponytail or a teased flip like Sandra Dee. I told Caroline how we had primped as usual in front of the broken kitchen mirror that night and started walking to the village. We stopped at a little shop on our way to buy sodas, or maybe it was breath mints. The shopkeeper, Mrs. Finnegan, looked at us and clucked her tongue.

"I hate to tell you girls, but there's no dance tonight," she said. "The president of the United States, John Fitzgerald Kennedy, was shot today. Everything is canceled."

Just five months earlier President Kennedy had visited his ancestral home in Dunganstown, County Wexford, arriving in Ireland mere hours after delivering his historic *"Ich bin ein Berliner"* speech in divided Germany. He had vowed to return to us soon, promising next time to bring his wife, Jackie, and their two children.

We had no television at home—no electricity, even—but two days after the shooting in Dallas, Texas, my whole family spent hours huddled around Dad's cheap battery-operated radio to listen as President Kennedy's funeral Mass, then the long procession to Arlington National Cemetery, and his graveside service were all broadcast across the Atlantic. I remembered catching the faint echo of hoofbeats three thousand miles away as the horse-drawn caisson carried the fallen president to his final resting place. And then came the muted roar of fifty military jets flying overhead in tribute. It wasn't that sound but the stillness that followed that made me feel connected for the first time in my life to a vast world beyond our small, rural corner of Ireland. Nothing this big had ever happened in my memory. I sensed that this sadness I felt was but a stitch in a tapestry more vast and intricate than any of us could possibly imagine.

Now I was telling President Kennedy's little girl how my father had come to our room that night, as he usually did for bedtime prayers, kneeling as he always did on the hard concrete floor, and how he offered up our daily rosary to the soul of President Kennedy and to his grieving family. "Peace be with them," he murmured as we finished our final round of three Hail Marys, one Our Father, and a Glory Be. *Peace be with them*, I echoed. I went to bed wondering what their lives would be like now.

I fell silent and saw tears falling down Caroline's cheeks. She was very quiet for a few moments then spoke up in a clear voice meant to reassure me she was all right.

"I was just saying a little prayer for him," she said, wiping her eyes.

"That's good, Caroline," I said. "I'll say one for him, too."

I couldn't know then, mere days into my new job, how thoroughly I would be swept up into this most royal of American families. How their everyday life would also become mine, my heart lifted by the powerful love they shared, and shattered by the unimaginable tragedies they endured. That I would someday tuck a piece of Caroline's wedding cake in my freezer, or teach her brother how to ride a bike. I had no inkling that their beloved mother would play such an important part in shaping the woman I was yet to become. That not only my life, but my very character, would be transformed not by where I was when it happened, but after.

Five years passed, then ten, then fifty.

And now, I'm finally ready to tell my other Kennedy story.

ONE

Meeting Madam

O n a chilly fall Thursday morning in 1964, I stood beneath the green awning at the entrance to an elegant prewar apartment house at the corner of Fifth Avenue and Eighty-fifth Street. Central Park was right across the street, trees ablaze in full autumn glory, and I could see the grand steps of the Metropolitan Museum of Art just down the block. After almost a year in New York, I was starting to become familiar with the city's landmarks, but the sense of awe that I was actually living here now was as fresh as it had been the day I stepped off the plane that had carried me from Ireland to John F. Kennedy International Airport. No one back home would ever believe that an uneducated immigrant farm girl was now moments away from meeting one of the most sophisticated and admired women in the world. I felt like a peasant about to have a private audience with the queen. What would Jacqueline Kennedy make of me? Pure Irish luck had landed me this interview, and all I could do now was pray that it would carry me through.

I swiped my clammy palms across my cheap, tatty coat and caught sight of the clunky black shoes I instantly wished I hadn't worn, not that I had so many others to choose from in my sparse wardrobe. I patted my head to make sure no stray hairs had escaped from the bobby-pinned bun that I thought might make me look more grown-up and professional than my age and résumé disclosed. I felt dowdy as a park pigeon as all the smart young secretaries and career girls hurried by on the sidewalk in their pencil skirts and heels. *Christ almighty,* I scolded myself, *were you thinking the Kennedys would be hiring a milkmaid, now?* I faked a brave smile for the Secret Service agent who greeted me and ushered me to the elevator. He was the one I really had to thank for this golden opportunity: My cousin Jack Maloney was a New York City policeman who had been assigned to do crowd control outside Mrs. Kennedy's building, and he'd become pals with this particular agent, a Boston-born-and-bred Irishman in his sixties by the name of John James O'Leary, who preferred to be called Mugsy. Mugsy tipped off Jack that Mrs. Kennedy was looking for a nice Irish girl to fill a position as a live-in domestic on her staff.

"Here you are," Mugsy said now as the doors parted at the fifteenth floor and I stepped out. "Good luck." He pushed the down button and disappeared before my legs could heed the urgent message my brain was sending to turn and run. *What are you thinking? You don't belong here!* I found myself inside a small foyer.

The door leading to the apartment's grander main entryway opened, and an older woman in a black uniform greeted me in a soft Irish brogue. The familiar lilt did nothing to calm my nerves, though; on the contrary, I instantly took note that her accent was nowhere near as thick as my own. Nearly a year in New York had done nothing to change it. It was like a porridge that refused to thin no matter how much milk you poured into it. I was constantly being asked to repeat myself in America. What if Mrs. Kennedy couldn't understand a word I said?

The housekeeper led me down a hallway, past a large mirror hanging on the wall in a beautiful tortoiseshell frame. I stole an anxious glance at my reflection: I looked every bit as awkward as I felt. My dark brown hair fell nearly to my waist when it was down, but it was too straight and fine to make a good bun. I had a knack for styling hair, but today's effort, to my disappointment, tilted more toward biddy than ballerina. I could say the same about my figure. I'd been athletic and nicely toned when I'd left Ireland, to be sure, but the loneliness and sheer misery of my first job in America—the one I was now trying to escape—had sent me on a junk-food binge that pushed my weight up to nearly 180 pounds on my five-foot-seven-inch frame. I averted my glance from the big mirror, focusing instead on the small silver saber, ornately sheathed, that rested on the polished mahogany console table beneath the mirror. The Irish maid led me down the hall to a formal living room with soaring picture windows facing Fifth Avenue.

"Mrs. Kennedy will be with you shortly," she said before disappearing.

I stood alone in the middle of the large room, wondering how to place myself. Should I be waiting for her, back straight, eyes ahead, like a soldier reporting for duty? Something about the decor told me this wasn't that stiff a household—it was a cross between cozy and elegant, the green velvet sofa with cream piping more plumply inviting than imposing. I gazed out the tall windows at the magnificent view. Central Park's billion-gallon reservoir shimmered like a giant's rain puddle. I could see the hansom cabs lined up on the street far below, tiny horses waiting to take tiny tourists on carriage rides. Ladies with shopping bags and businessmen with briefcases hurried along Fifth Avenue. Manhattan suddenly seemed like a toy village.

I turned my attention back to the living room, my eyes gravitating to the treasures so casually and perfectly displayed— lacquered boxes and porcelain vases, fancy ashtrays, framed etchings and oil paintings hanging on the walls. In the corner by the doorway stood a life-size statue of a headless naked person, illuminated by its own spotlight. Instinctively, I drew my arms closer to my body. I could hear the sharp voice of my current employer in my head, hectoring me about my clumsiness. She wasn't entirely wrong, but her badgering made me nervous, and that, in turn, caused even more mishaps. She docked my wages for each one. My paycheck would never begin to cover the replacement cost of anything I accidentally broke, burned, or bleached at this address. *Calm down,* I told myself. If I made myself any more nervous than I already was, I would be too tongue-tied to even utter my name, much less answer any interview questions.

I decided I would perch daintily on the edge of the green sofa. Polite and poised, that would be the perfect note to strike! I sat, only to sink deeply into the down cushion. I was struggling to rearrange myself so I wouldn't look like Cleopatra lounging around in hopes of being fed a grape when a small boy with a mop of brown hair wandered into the room. A black-and-white cocker spaniel bounded after him.

"Hello," the boy greeted me politely. "I'm John. Do you want to see my dog do a trick?"

Both his grin and his energy were infectious. I smiled back and nodded.

"Sure!"

"Shannon!" he commanded. "Roll over!" Tail wagging, the dog flopped onto the silk Oriental rug and rolled over. "Roll over again!" John urged him. Shannon immediately obliged.

I was genuinely impressed. I'd grown up with a farm full of animals, forever chasing them down or being chased by them, it seemed, and here this little guy was practically P. T. Barnum before even his fourth birthday. He wasn't done. "Watch this," he said, taking a bone from his pocket and shoving it beneath one of the couch cushions.

"Shanny, get the bone!" John urged, the excitement in his voice sending the spaniel into what looked like a tail-wagging state of rapture, barking as he leaped up onto the sofa and began searching for his prize. The dog pawed furiously between the cushions until he found his bone and retrieved it.

I clapped my hands. "Wow, what a smart dog!" I exclaimed.

The little boy beamed with pride.

"Seriously, John," I went on, "that's no easy thing you've done there. You're a terrific dog trainer!"

"John, you're not letting that dog ruin my couch, are you?" I heard a woman softly chide. Neither of us had seen her slip into the room. I had no idea how long she'd been standing there. She stepped forward with a warm smile.

"Hi, I'm Mrs. Kennedy," she introduced herself, needlessly. We were the same height, I would come to find out, but with her regal bearing, she seemed taller. I self-consciously straightened my shoulders and sucked in my stomach as I rose to greet her. She wore a long turtleneck sweater, smartly belted around her narrow waist, with tailored slacks. I caught just a whisper of her perfume, something floral but light. I was surprised by how naturally elegant she was—no big flashing diamonds or movie-star makeup. I could immediately see the resemblance between mother and son; both of them had fair skin and wonderfully thick, wavy dark hair, but her brown eyes were as deep and unreadable as John's were open and guileless.

I had barely stammered out my introduction when she nodded and asked me her first question: "Can you start right away?"

I was dumbfounded. Had she just offered me the job, without so much as a single query about my qualifications? I would learn much later from the staff that she had been watching from the hallway the whole time I was chatting with John. Here I had been worried about having to undergo some rigorous interrogation and Secret Service check, but the truth was, I had just been vetted by a preschooler and his cocker spaniel.

"I don't know, I mean, I haven't told my employer anything, and I'll need to give her a few days' notice," I sputtered, wondering even as the words left my mouth why I felt the least bit of obligation to the bitter divorcée who had first hired me when I came to America months earlier. I was supposed to be her governess, but what she really wanted, it had turned out, was someone she could berate on a daily basis now that her browbeaten husband had left. I could do nothing right. My very existence seemed to exasperate the woman I'll call Mrs. C.

"Could you tell her today, and start tomorrow?" Mrs. Kennedy suggested.

"I suppose I could, but she'll likely get angry and not give me a good reference," I fretted aloud.

Mrs. Kennedy smiled the Mona Lisa half-smile that so bewitched every photographer who ever tried to capture the "real" her. "You don't need a reference," she pointed out. "You've already got the job!"

We agreed I would return the next morning with my suitcase. It all seemed strangely matter-of-fact, more like I was watching a dream than having it, much less actually *living* it. I suppose I was just so filled with relief to be freed from my awful situation with Mrs. C that it didn't even fully register at first who had just rescued me. My self-esteem by then had sunk so low that I couldn't even congratulate myself for having just landed the most coveted job in America for a girl of my station.

⟋⟍

Arriving back the next morning at 1040—everyone's shorthand, I soon learned, for the 1040 Fifth Avenue residence—Mrs. Kennedy's chief of staff and personal secretary, Nancy Tuckerman, gave me the rundown of my position as personal assistant to Mrs. Kennedy: I would attend to Mrs. Kennedy and also fill in as needed when the English governess, Maud Shaw, was off or on vacation. I would have Thursdays off but was expected to work every other weekend and all holidays (except Christmas Day after the midafternoon meal). I would get a couple of weeks' vacation each summer, and Mrs. Kennedy would provide a free round-trip plane ticket home to Ireland so I could visit my family. I would also be regularly traveling with Mrs. Kennedy and the kids—to Cape Cod for the summer, to New Jersey for weekends of horseback riding, to Colorado for skiing, and to Palm Beach for winter break, plus any little jaunts in between. The longtime assistant I was replacing would continue to accompany Mrs. Kennedy on her overseas trips, though. Like the cook, waitress, and governess, I would live in the residence. I would be paid seventy-five dollars a week. I was to address Mrs. Kennedy as "Madam."

It all sounded so overwhelming, as if I were taking on not merely a new job, but also a whole new life—one I could never have imagined and had no idea how to carry off. Was I expected to ski?! Wintertime where I grew up meant sliding across frozen lakes in our shoes, or taking an old cardboard box out to ride down the small, empty country roads when they turned into treacherous ribbons of ice. Ireland never lacked for rolling hills, and we made the most of them as kids. Who needed proper ice skates or sleds, let alone a pair of skis? As for my indoor duties, well, I could make a nice bed, to be sure, or happily entertain small children for hours at a time. But the truth was, I had no professional training and not the slightest clue what being a personal assistant even meant—yet now I was to do it for one of the most glamorous women in the world? I didn't have that kind of polish, and no idea how to fake it! The only one who seemed to have any confidence whatsoever in my untested abilities was Mrs. Kennedy herself. *God save the both of us*, I thought anxiously.

The servants' quarters were in a hallway just off the kitchen. My pristine white bedroom was small yet cozy, with a clock radio and lamp on the nightstand. There was a soft armchair with a small table beside it where I could pen my brief and sporadic letters home. I wasn't much of a correspondent. There was a little sink with a mirrored medicine cabinet there in the bedroom. (When Madam later decided to redecorate the servants' wing, I was thrilled to be able to choose what I liked from the wallpaper samples her decorator selected. I had never been able to put any personal stamp on the bedroom I shared with my brothers and sisters in Ireland, and with girlish impulse, I decided on a pattern of sweet little pink posies for my bedroom at 1040—not realizing how claustrophobic I was going to feel once a matching bedspread and new pink carpet were in place, too. It wasn't until I had daughters of my own that I saw that what I had done was basically give myself the little girl's dream room I had never had in my hardscrabble childhood.) The help shared a large bathroom just steps down the hall, and we also had use of a small lounge off the kitchen where we could take our breaks or relax after the workday was done.

Besides me and Maud, my new coworkers would include May, the Irishwoman who had shown me in and served as waitress, plus a series of mostly sourpuss cooks who never lasted long, and then Charley, who did the heavier, janitorial-type chores, like vacuuming or polishing all the floors and cleaning the half dozen toilets. May was well into her forties, but she had this innocent, childlike quality to her that you couldn't help but like. Maud and Charley were both in their sixties. Charley was a flamboyant gay bachelor from Galway who reminded me of a little leprechaun the way he waggled his behind when he walked. He combed black shoe polish through his full head of white hair to give it a salt-and-pepper look and favored patent leather shoes. He was a charmer with the gift of gab, and I took a liking to him right away. Maud was a different story: Maybe it was her posh English accent, or the air of authority she no doubt needed as a nanny, but I could feel her disdain instantly. She didn't seem to mingle much with the rest of the staff, either, even preferring to take meals in her room rather than in the kitchen or break room with everyone else.

After meeting them all, I was put under the tutelage of the

longtime assistant I was replacing. Providencia Paredes had begun working for Mrs. Kennedy in Washington, D.C., a few years before President Kennedy was elected, and then moved into the White House with the family. Provi's primary task was managing Mrs. Kennedy's large wardrobe, keeping everything in like-new condition, properly rotated by the season, each outfit meticulously assembled according to the occasion. Provi also made sure every ensemble was perfectly accessorized to Mrs. Kennedy's specifications, down to matching slippers and bathrobes for every nightdress. I would also pack and unpack Mrs. Kennedy's leather Louis Vuitton suitcases for each trip. It was Provi who had selected the pink Chanel-style suit and pillbox hat for Dallas that November day.

Both the pride Provi took in her work and the attention to detail she gave it were evident from the minute she began showing me what to do. At forty, Provi was twice my age, but she didn't look it; she was busty but trim and compact, with smooth brown skin and neatly coiffed hair. Originally from the Dominican Republic, she spoke with a Spanish accent every bit as indecipherable as my Irish brogue, and we spent a good portion of every conversation asking each other to repeat things.

Provi may have been diminutive, but she was as bossy as a five-star general. And she may have been a servant herself, but like Maud Shaw, Provi radiated a sense of what came across to me as entitlement, almost. Like she was a partner to this life of

18

luxury, not merely propping it up. I couldn't quite decide whether I should envy her aplomb or resent her airs.

As she set about showing me the ropes, I sensed a hint of insult and resentment on her part that Madam had deemed someone so green and unsophisticated a worthy successor to her. Looking back, I can hardly blame her: She was a titan being replaced by a teenager, after all.

"Not like that! Watch me and pay attention this time!" became the refrain that snapped me out of my girlish daydreams as she overexplained even the simplest chores.

Our first lesson was back in the laundry room at the ironing board. I knew how to iron already, but Provi wasn't about to move on until she was certain that I knew how to iron her way. Madam's sheets were to be changed daily, and her nightgowns were to be freshly ironed and set out for her each evening. She had quite a collection: There were movie-star peignoirs in satin and lace, timelessly simple gowns in crisp cottons or linen, and cute, flirty numbers like the short canary yellow one with a bow on each shoulder. Provi handed me a long-sleeved cotton nightgown to practice on. I swiped the hot iron across the wrinkles and handed it back.

Provi scowled.

"You missed some," she scolded. "Go slower, and press down harder."

I couldn't imagine Jacqueline Kennedy settling into her bed

at night only to leap right back out in horror because there were some wrinkles in her nightgown. Who was going to look anyway, besides Provi? I wisely kept this argument to myself and had another go at the ironing board. At least this wasn't the disaster my first ironing session with Mrs. C had been, when I hadn't known to remove the protective plastic cover from the ironing board first, and ended up melting it into one of her favorite blouses.

Provi's ironing lesson wasn't nearly as bad as her tutorial on the care of Madam's collection of leather gloves, which turned out to involve rubbing down the pigskin with cleaning fluid.

"Provi, that's awful dangerous," I ventured as the toxic fumes filled the laundry room, making my eyes and lungs burn.

"Well, you have to open a window or turn on the fan," Provi said matter-of-factly, doing neither. Once the gloves were clean, she continued, they needed to be spread out on a white towel and massaged with baby powder to make them nice and slippy again. *And then you wait for the ambulance to come take you to the hospital*, I thought. Once my apprenticeship was over and Provi was gone, I fully intended to put those gloves in with the dry cleaning.

Provi's reputation for being a high-handed perfectionist was well established at 1040, and I spent tedious hours watching her demonstrate all manner of simple chores that my teenaged brain assured me I could accomplish in half the time with half the effort. It was excruciating to fritter away two hours "learning" how to vacuum the white tile floor in Madam's bathroom when there wasn't a speck of dust to be seen in the first place. Provi could spy a single strand of hair hiding along a baseboard from across the room.

"You have to check," she insisted, not satisfied until I had crouched down to examine my efforts tile by tile. One afternoon when I had finally ironed a nightgown to her military standards and went to put it away, Provi snatched it right back with a sharp sigh of disgust. "You didn't fold it right," she complained. *What do I ever do right?* I thought, my defense mechanism from Mrs. C's endless harping kicking in automatically before I could remind myself that at the end of the day Provi's servant boot camp was for my own good. I anxiously wondered if Madam was as exacting as Provi was, though, and how long it would be before the former first lady realized what a bumbling impostor she had put in such a choice position on her staff. I folded the nightgown again, concentrating on each step as if my life depended on it.

I was somewhat relieved to find out that it wasn't just me who was rankled by Provi's superiority. The Secret Service men assigned to protect John and Caroline throughout their childhood often hung out with the help in the kitchen or break room when they were changing shifts or hoping for a free sandwich or cup of tea. Mugsy, the one who had gotten me my job, took particular delight in needling Provi, reminding her that she was a lame duck and that young Kitty, as he called me, was running the house now. "Kitty, is the Mexican princess bossing you around?" he would ask, managing to insult Provi's seniority and nationality in one fell swoop. She would fire some disparaging remark right back at him.

Their constant sniping was free entertainment, at least for all the Irish help. It's true that we do love a good fight.

Madam stayed out of the domestic dramas playing out in her kitchen and back hallway, but she wasn't clueless about them, I soon discovered. In the running dialogue in my head, I was cheeky as you please and mouthed off to Provi all the time, but in reality, I was a scared little rabbit whose instinct was to scamper away and hide if I sensed that trouble was afoot, or if I simply felt overwhelmed. Being Madam's personal assistant didn't allow for hesitation: I was expected to plunge right into the busy routines of 1040, not ease my way tentatively into the current of life there. In my own element, I was a sociable girl, but the more I worried about whether I would fit in, the more likely I was to withdraw. The natural chattiness and ease Madam had seen in me when I had been left alone in the living room with John wasn't as evident as I tried to get my bearings, and Madam quickly noticed. She seemed concerned about me settling in and not being chased off the way, I gathered, some previous heirs to Provi's throne had been.

"How are you making out?" she asked me kindly when we were alone one day. "Is she all right with you?"

"Oh, yes, Madam," I hastened to assure her. "Everything's fine, thank you." Sure, Provi was nitpicky, but when you came right down to it, she was annoying, not cruel. I could live with that.

Provi's primary domain—soon to be mine—was Madam's closets. The bedroom walk-in was big but jam-packed with Madam's everyday dresses, pants, skirts, and blouses, all arranged according to color. Lots of clothes still had their tags from Saks Fifth Avenue or Bergdorf Goodman and would eventually go unworn into the big bags Madam filled with clothes she planned to donate to the thrift shop or church charity. Fashionable pocketbooks and the roomy satchels she favored were lined up on the shelves, along with an array of beautiful hatboxes. Drawers or special fabric-lined boxes held accessories such as her signature gloves or the colorful head scarves that were considered the height of fashion then, no matter what the weather.

Fine as they were, I thought it must be confusing to have so many outfits. *And why so many of the same thing, some even in the same color?* I wondered, taking in the array of cream turtleneck sweaters alone. Oh, but it wasn't the clothes I coveted. The shoes were what set my heart racing. A single pair of shoes was an extravagance in my big family when I was growing up. Most of our clothes were hand-me-downs from relatives in America who sent care packages a couple of times a year, and none of Uncle Pat and Aunt Rose's girls wore the same size shoe as my sister Briege and me. We always had to stuff paper or rags in the toes of the ones that were too big, or suffer the pinching from the ones that were too small. I don't remember ever having a pair that actually fit. One of my favorite pastimes once I got to New York City was to window-shop for shoes at the fashionable shops on the Upper East Side. Madam's closet could rival any of them.

I had never seen such a dazzling selection of shoes! There were enough to fill a high-end boutique—leather boots in classic cognac, London-look ones in mod white and sexy black, pumps in every color and heel, elegantly casual loafers, spotless sneakers for morning jogs around the reservoir, and a pair of ivory flip-flops with a big leather flower separating the toes. The latter, I came to see, were a favorite, often hidden beneath a long, flowing caftan or maxidress when she hosted small dinner parties with old friends, like the men from President Kennedy's trusted inner circle who would appear now and then as a group to check in on her, all of them talking and smoking and drinking and laughing, remembering deep into the night.

As I surveyed the closet, trying to memorize where everything went, Provi took out a pair of size ten pumps and turned them over to show me an X carved into each leather sole. "You have to do this to every new pair that comes into the house," Provi instructed. The discreet slashes, she explained, kept Madam from slipping on slick marble floors. It about killed me the first time I dutifully knifed the bottom of an exquisite kid pump—I would have felt less heartsick had I been told to go up the block and vandalize a masterpiece at the Met instead. Less shocking but more intriguing to me was the discovery of a quarter-inch lift affixed to one heel on each pair of Madam's shoes, apparently meant to compensate for one leg being slightly shorter than the other. No one would have ever guessed: Even in her stocking feet, she had flawlessly beautiful posture.

⌘

Shoes were actually the very first thing Madam and I bonded over.

Mrs. Tuckerman had provided a crisp white uniform when I was hired, and I used a good bit of my final hard-won paycheck from Mrs. C to splurge on new shoes to match the uniform. I somehow convinced myself that the thick-soled nurse's shoes I bought were as stylish as they were practical as I pulled them on the first morning I woke up at 1040. At least they were nice and cushy. I didn't even have to bother with anklets or stockings. Off to the kitchen I padded to pick up Madam's tray of tea, toast, a soft-boiled egg, and the daily newspapers: Bringing her breakfast in bed at eight o'clock was my first official duty each day. I was nervous. Was I supposed to shake her if she didn't awaken when I entered? Sing out a cheery "Good morning!" or wait until I was spoken to first? I had ironed enough nightgowns to know, at least, that she wouldn't be waiting for me like my previous employer did: in her birthday suit. My hands were already clammy as I stood outside the bedroom door and lightly knocked before entering.

"Good morning, Madam," I murmured as I set the tray down and began opening the shutters. Clear fall light spilled across her queen bed as she stirred. Her corner bedroom faced the broad sweep of Fifth Avenue and Central Park along the front, and the narrower, quieter Eighty-fifth Street to the side. The room was wonderfully tranquil.

But as I walked from window to window I became aware of a persistent little squeaking sound.

The realization that it was coming from my feet, which were perspiring against the rubber of my new shoes, made me more nervous than I already was and only amplified the squeaks that resulted from my every step. I was mortified. I glanced over and saw that Madam was fully awake and propped against her pillows, settling in with her tea and papers. There was no way she *couldn't* have heard the squeaks, and I was sure she assumed the worst. I hurried into the bathroom, hoping she would think I was merely arranging towels or something, and frantically rummaged through her cupboards until I found the tin of talcum powder I was looking for. I sat down on the closed toilet lid and thoroughly dusted the inside of each nurse shoe, praying the chalk would absorb the moisture from my feet and squelch the humiliating soundtrack.

Mission accomplished, I hurried back into the master bed-room, my shoes blissfully quiet. All that powder felt silky on my feet, too. No cheap drugstore stuff in that bathroom.

My relief was short-lived when I noticed something floating around my feet at ground level, like a little white cloud. Madam was busy with her breakfast by then and hadn't noticed what I now spotted—powder marks all over her carpet. I took a few ten-tative steps and saw white puffs shooting out of my shoes. I darted back into the bathroom, shutting the door this time, and sat on the toilet lid again, trying to figure out what to do, now that my shoes were emitting what looked like smoke. I couldn't go out there again! She would know I had gotten into her powder! I was going to be fired before lunch on my very first day. What a bum-bling, hopeless mess I was, and now I couldn't even run away to save face, because I was trapped in Jacqueline Kennedy's bath-room. I put my head in my hands and started laughing uncontrol-lably.

"Kathy, is everything all right?" I heard the door open, and the worry in Madam's voice as she took in the sight of me with my face still buried in my hands, shoulders shaking. "What's wrong?" she asked kindly.

I was too embarrassed to answer, and in the midst of my gig-gling fit I wouldn't have been able to get an intelligible sentence out anyway, so I jumped up and ran past her, shooting puffs of powder from my shoes as I fled. I was losing too much powder, though, and the squeaking noises were back, sounding louder and more urgent as I sprinted to my room. I collapsed on the bed, burying my face in the pillow to muffle my laughter.

"Kathy?" There she was again. Madam tapped on the closed door.

I had no choice but to open it. She stepped in, her perfectly arched brows furrowed with concern. The look on her face quickly turned to bewilderment when she realized that I was laughing, not sobbing. Unless I wanted a Secret Service escort to the loony bin, it was time to come clean. As I started to explain the whole story, Madam burst into laughter, which sent me into another spasm of hysterics, and by the time I led her into the hallway to point out my telltale trail of powdered footprints, both of us had tears running down our cheeks.

The rest of the staff took turns peeking around the corner, trying to see what was so amusing. We finally composed ourselves, and Madam was still chuckling when she ventured into the kitchen, where the rest of the staff were clamoring to know what had just happened with the new girl.

"Oh, that Kath is just too funny," I overheard her say.

TWO

Back in Inniskeen

Inis Caoin.

In Gaelic, it means "peaceful island," but that makes life in my home village of Inniskeen sound far easier than it was. Ireland has always been brilliant at public relations that way—all green hills and leprechauns and stone castles—but even from the beginning, when St. Daigh founded a monastery there in the sixth century, Inniskeen had a rough go of it: The Vikings plundered and burned the place to the ground not once, but twice. Fourteen centuries later, not terribly much had changed in the verdant green countryside where my family scratched out a living on the farm my father still plowed by horse even as men were being launched into outer space aboard rocket ships. The 1960s would turn out to be a decade that changed the whole world forever, the most thrilling era of the century to be a teenager, but I had no inkling of that, much less of where I would end up on the invisible game board. Time was more inclined to drag its feet than march briskly forward in the corner of Ireland we knew, tucked tight against the border with the restive north.

My family—all ten of us—lived in a three-room stone cottage with no running water or electricity, content to do so because we knew nothing else. "If you don't have it, you don't need it," my mother was fond of saying. She was right, really, when you think about it, and I grew up happy enough with my lot, never the one to foster grand ambitions or dreams of a future anywhere else. We knew how to scrimp and scrub and sacrifice, and we worked very hard for what we got. We were poor, but there were poorer than us, and we had land—good land, at that. I assumed my life would always be right there in County Monaghan, as predictable as the trains that clattered past on the tracks behind our house and doubled as our clock: The morning one at nine o'clock meant it was time to head to school; the last one at half past ten signaled bedtime.

I was the middle of eight children for Jack and Maggie Smith, the four eldest stair-stepped a year apart, the youngest, two. Patrick came first, then Michael, my sister Bridget, me, then Mary, the youngest girl and darling of the family, followed by John, Jim, and finally the baby, Owen. Owney was a premature baby, so tiny he weighed barely four pounds on the neighbor's borrowed turkey scale. Mam would send me into the village to ask the pub keeper for empty pints of whiskey, which she fashioned into baby bottles by stretching rubber nipples over the top. She'd rinse the bottles out with boiling water from the pot kept hanging over the open fireplace we used for cooking. The setup was more like a permanent indoor campsite than a proper stove, but that steady flame kept us all warm and fed 'til we were grown and gone. Owney thrived on the milk he drank fresh from our dairy cows, and if our crude sterilization method ever left a nip of whiskey lingering in his bottles, it was all well and good. Owney was a happy baby who clearly didn't mind an unintended nightcap.

From the time we were toddlers old enough to scatter chicken feed, we all pitched in to work the farm and keep our busy household running. Before and after school, my brothers, sisters, and I would be tending to the animals or trekking across the fields to fetch buckets of water from the River Fain to do the dishes and laundry, or from the well that supplied our drinking water, so cold and delicious, from an underground spring. Laundry was an ongoing chore, everything scrubbed by hand on a washboard with a bar of soap, then hung to dry outside if the weather was fair—less often than not in our misty hills—or indoors on the maze of clotheslines that crisscrossed high above our kitchen table, raised and lowered with a string pulley like Venetian blinds. Nothing ever got soft. Our towels dried hard and rough as sandpaper. And if by chance your clothes *were* drying outside, you had to watch out that they weren't snatched away by the Gypsies—we called them travelers—who would pass through in the summertime in caravans that looked like the covered wagons you see in old westerns, only painted in bright colors instead and drawn by magnificent horses. I don't know whether the travelers bred those horses or stole them, but they were always so beautiful, more like sleek Thoroughbreds than the shaggy workhorses we knew.

I used to spot the bands of travelers camping down by the river, and they would come up to the house to ask if Mam needed any pots repaired. For a few coins, they would fix a hole in a tin pot with a washer and small screw, sealing it so expertly you'd never have so much as a drop of water leak from it again. Mam was happy to do business with them until the time one of the women distracted her by asking for a bit of milk for the baby in her arms, and while Mam was getting it, don't you know the Gypsies went and stole all our clothes off the line. They were long gone by the time we noticed, and more than likely our freshly laundered hand-me-downs ended up for sale at a swap meet in another village a day or two later. That was about as exciting as things in Inniskeen ever got, unless you counted the murderous nights when a fox slipped through the rickety door to our hen-house. The ensuing commotion would wake us all, and Dad would go flying out the door to give chase in his nightshirt, armed with a broom or Mam's big wooden potato masher. Mam would find the bloody feathers of the latest victim in an empty nest the next morning when she went to gather the day's eggs. Dad used to carry crates of eggs on his back five miles up through the fields into Northern Ireland, where he got a better price for them. The eggs our chickens laid were strictly for market, and the same went for the pigs in our sty, whose bacon, pork chops, and ham we never got to enjoy, either. The life of subsistence farmers is always more about sacrifice than bounty.

None of the farms surrounding Inniskeen could afford all the modern machinery, tools, or hired hands needed to be self-sustaining, so we all relied on neighborly goodwill to survive. Farmers helped each other when it was time to plant or harvest the crops, with everyone pitching in and moving in a circle from farm to farm until every acre had been plowed or harrowed. The grown-ups started working before the sun came up and kept at it 'til there was no longer the light to toil by. There was never any letup for illness or injury, unless it was crippling or grave. I can remember Dad being driven nearly mad once by the pain from an infected tooth, his jaw swollen and throbbing. He would come in at the end of the day and just slump down at the dinner table with his head in his hands. We couldn't afford a visit to the druggist, let alone the dentist, and a farm doesn't hold still while its owner takes to bed, so all poor Dad could do was carry on as usual for day after agonizing day until the rotting molar finally fell out. Farmwork wears people down too soon, even the healthy ones. It was doubly hard on Dad, since he and my brothers also pitched in to run Aunt Bridge's place as well. Her husband, Teddy, had been a carpenter by trade, but severe asthma kept him indoors wheezing by the fire most of the time. It shocks me now to realize that my own father was probably barely even forty when he started complaining of chest pains. He would grow so short of breath carrying two heavy jugs in from milking that he would have to stop and sit on the low stone wall to rest for a few minutes. One time, I came home to find him sitting in the kitchen while Mam knelt on the concrete floor, bathing his grotesquely swollen feet in a pail of cool water.

"It's coming from his heart," she said somberly, looking up.

As winter approached and our hay, barley, and oats were all threshed, one of the last tasks left in the fields each year was to gather the potatoes. Our old brown horse, Nelly, would pull the plow, with Dad steering her through the rows while the children followed in aprons made of mail sacks, miserably plunging our gloveless hands into the freezing mud to pluck up the spuds one by one. My fingers would hurt with cold, then eventually go numb. When the harvest season was over and done with, Dad would walk into Inniskeen to settle his bill at the general store owned by Sam Paugh and his two brothers. Sam kept a big ledger of every single item everyone purchased over the previous year. He would add up the columns under our name, and Dad would usually leave without a penny, sometimes even carrying over a small balance. All that work, and we were poor again.

We were all masters of the rotation game: My parents had to share a single pair of glasses. If Dad wanted to read a paper by the weak gauzy glow of our methylated spirits lantern, then Mam couldn't darn the holes in our socks at the same time. Also shared was the single toothbrush we owned. Who had left it where was a running argument in a house with ten mouths. We used plain water or baking soda to brush with, except for the time when I decided to try a traditional Irish method of whitening teeth I'd heard about, and stuck the communal toothbrush up the chimney to rub it thoroughly in soot. (The only way soot makes your teeth look whiter, I can report, is by turning the rest of your mouth black by contrast.)

With such a big family, the housework was never ending, even in such cramped quarters. You would think the most dreaded chore would be washing the dishes without benefit of a sink or faucet, but seeing as how there was never that much to eat, there wasn't that much to clean, either. Every day, Mam baked a loaf of dark soda bread, setting it out to cool on the stone wall, where we had to mind that the chickens didn't get to it before we did. It smelled so good, I longed to just steal it myself.

But like everything else we had, the bread had to be rationed carefully. A fresh, chewy hunk served as breakfast in the morning, and we were allowed to take another piece to school for lunch. We smeared it sparingly with the sweet cream butter we churned by hand and then rolled into tiny balls, each of us allotted one ball a day for our bread and one for our potatoes. Potatoes were our mainstay—mashed, boiled, or fire roasted for dinner every night. Gleaned from the crop we grew to sell, we always had plenty of potatoes.

Meat and fish appeared only rarely on our plates, though Dad and the boys would sometimes succeed in poaching wild salmon from the river during spawning season, using crude fishing poles made from sticks and hooks. Dad would cut the fat salmon into pieces, which would be stored in a pail down the well to keep cool, and we would make it last as long as we could. Dad caught eels, too, which he liked to toss on the kitchen fire until the skin crackled, but none of the rest of us would touch the horrid things. I would have much rather seen a lamb chop sizzling on the coals from our small sheep flock. We kept a goat, too, whose milk was mixed in with the cows' because it enriched it just enough to win us a higher grade and better price from the creamery. That was strictly forbidden, of course, but everyone did it.

Even in the rain, Dad did all our milking by hand out in the fields where the cows grazed. It was my job to bring the herd in before dark to bed down in their cowshed. Unlike American barns, the cowsheds that dot rural Ireland aren't big stand-alone buildings set away from the farmhouses. They're attached right to the house, like a wing for the in-laws. As luck would have it, I shared a bedroom wall with our herd, whose loud chuffing, groaning, and lowing provided the bass section to the chorus of snores and murmurs from my brothers and sisters as the whole lot of us settled in to sleep at night. Mam and Dad had the other bedroom. As we got bigger, stacking all us kids in shared bunk beds like loaves of bread in a baker's rack became less manage-able, and the two older boys gradually migrated across the road to sleep at our childless Aunt Bridge and Uncle Teddy's house. I might've gotten a better night's rest if the cows had followed, too.

Accustomed as we were to getting by with so little, we could count on a magnificent windfall: a big package from America, twice a year. Dad's older brother, Pat, and his wife, Rose, had im-migrated to America and lived in New York City with their chil-dren. At Christmastime, they would send little toys like bubbles and coloring books, cap guns, paper dolls, and mouth harps the Americans called harmonicas and we knew as French fiddles. Plus fat barbershop-pole candy canes for each of us. Once there was even a beautiful golden-haired doll for us girls to share. She wore a white pinafore and bloomers over her pink dress, and a frilly bonnet framed her sweet porcelain face. If you laid her down, her blue eyes would close, then flutter open again when you picked her up. Of course, we didn't know when we were little that the gifts came from our American relatives; Uncle Teddy would play Santa Claus and bring them over in a big sack for us on Christmas Eve.

Christmas Day, we'd all go to Mass, and our festivities would wrap up with Dad making his single exception to the usual for-market-only rule about the turkeys we raised. Big, dumb, and defensive those birds were, with a vicious streak that left my legs scratched and bloodied on more than one occasion. I savored our Christmas dinner with no remorse at all.

Our second annual gift box from New York would come in the spring, full of hand-me-down clothes from our American cousins. We girls loved to play fashion show with all our new dresses, and always gave Mary, as the smallest, first pick of what to model as we twirled and preened for each other. Since there was only a lone cousin close to the size Briege and I wore, the box would yield just one winter coat that fit us both. Briege would wear it to early Mass on Sunday, and then hand it off to me to wear to later services. On the walk to school, we traded it back and forth, depending on who was coldest.

Each morning all of us who were old enough would set off for the schoolhouse a mile and a half away, carrying the books we hadn't studied because we had no light to read by, and the home-work we didn't do because paper was a luxury we couldn't afford. The perpetual rain would soak us to the bone by the time we arrived, and the holes in our worn Wellingtons ensured that even the soles of our feet would be wet and cold. My second-oldest brother, Mick, was in charge of gathering sticks to light the fire in the school's big black cast-iron stove, which was meant to warm the whole class but in truth mostly warmed the headmaster, Mr. Mullen, who would stand square in front of the fire all day, toasting his own backside while blocking the heat from his shivering pupils.

Mick was the cleverest one of our bunch, able to rattle off answers in any subject, but he was as mischievous as he was smart, so that shot any chance the Smith clan had at impressing Mr. Mullen instead of earning his daily disdain. "There's no point in calling on any of you," Mr. Mullen would often say, fixing his beady eyes on the row of us, "because you wouldn't know the answer anyway." Schools decided back then which children to send on to high school, and the fact of the matter was, the poorer ones were less likely to go, even if they were deemed scholarly enough, because they were sorely needed to help support their families. I remember one day when Patrick, my oldest brother, accidentally knocked the map of the world onto the classroom floor when his shoulder brushed the wall on his way out the door at lunchtime. He hastened to pick it up, embarrassed by his own twelve-year-old clumsiness, but Mr. Mullen couldn't just let Packy be.

"You'd be better off at home helping your father out," the teacher hissed low in Packy's face. The underlying message was meant for all of us to hear: Children like us would never amount to much and weren't worth the trouble. We hated Mr. Mullen in that pure and thorough way that only children can, and in turn, he demonstrated his contempt for us with a leather strap that stung even more than his words.

When I was in seventh grade, our parents had decided it was time for Briege and me to quit school and go to work full-time. We were needed to help make ends meet at home. I didn't mind at all. It was just how things were.

An informal barter system was what kept even the poorest farms in Inniskeen struggling along. My father, for example, might borrow a mower to cut the grass from a neighbor who accepted the added muscle of our horse another day in return. Children were loaned out as well, with two girls and one boy being equal to the labor of one grown man. Dad's best friend, Putty, would let Dad borrow his hired hand in exchange for sending some kids over to pick bushels of berries or yank up weeds. Children were considered better suited to chores that involved a lot of stooping over. I hated being loaned out like the plow horse, especially when it came to digging up potatoes. Sometimes a farm wife might offer to feed us supper, but that was it.

Putty regularly asked Dad to send me and Briege over to lend a hand, and to our despair, Dad always obliged, never knowing what it was Putty was really after. It started when I was around twelve, and Putty suddenly jumped out from behind a haystack as I walked past, grabbing my leg. "Gotcha!!" he cried, baring his brown tobacco teeth in a hyena laugh as I screamed and wriggled, finally freeing myself of his groping hands by sinking my own teeth into his arm. He laughed again as I took off. "Oh, Kathleen, when you get old enough, I'm gonna marry ya!" he called after me. He wasn't the only dirty old man who liked to sneak up from behind to try to put his hands where they didn't belong, or pull young girls close for a slobbery kiss. It was about as likely to happen as not. Briege and I were too scared and embarrassed to ever tell. Instead, we formed our own security system, sticking as close together as possible and deploying a swift kick or sharp elbow as needed. Mam had never warned us about this, or told us what to do. She wasn't the type to have those kinds of conversations. I knew she loved us and all, but Mam had been closed off for as long as I could remember, the kind of wife and mother who gets remembered as hardworking and dutiful. And what could she do about it anyway?

Briege had always been good with a needle and thread, and after we left school, she quickly landed a good job at a coat factory in a town not far from Inniskeen. She also did some light housekeeping at the parish rectory house. When Briege fell off her bike and got sidelined with a broken wrist, I was sent to the rectory in her place. The fussy old priest came to me with a strange rubber bag and told me to fill it with hot water before I left and place it between the sheets to warm his bed. I had never seen, much less used, a hot-water bottle before, but it seemed simple enough, and I dutifully followed Father's instructions so he could settle into his nice toasty covers that cold winter's night. What happened next came to me secondhand, since the priest himself had no wish to ever see or speak to me again, but from what I gathered, Father tucked himself in and quickly sprang back out again, bellowing first in shock, then fury. Far from the cozy nest he had expected to snuggle down into, he had discovered himself swaddled in a freezing wet wad of sheets: I hadn't screwed the cap of the water bottle on straight, and the priest's bed had been flooded, soaked through to the mattress, which, of course, took ages to dry in Ireland's perpetual damp. Briege with one arm was deemed more competent than I was with two, and that ended my first job outside my own home.

Good thing for me, word of my shortcomings as a domestic didn't spread, and soon I was hired by a well-to-do family to help out around the house. Their home was the grandest one in Inniskeen, a mansion by local standards; Mr. O'Rourke owned the mill where all the farmers sent their grain to be processed. The O'Rourkes enjoyed all the modern amenities within reach of the Irish upper classes at the time—indoor plumbing, lights that turned on with a flick of the switch, an actual kitchen with a refrigerator and range, and a heating system that kept every room warm even in freezing weather. There were matching linens when I made the beds, and the windows were all dressed up like debutantes with their fancy drapes. I helped Mrs. O'Rourke and her daughter, Rose, with all the chores. Rose's mother was quite bossy, but Rose never openly challenged her mum and went about her work without complaint. She was responsible for doing the laundry, among other things, and we would spend long hours ironing all the clothes, first dipping the collars and cuffs of her father's shirts in the starch we made from potato water. When we washed the windows, Rose would perch on the sill and I would lower the window on her legs to hold her down while she hung out to clean the outside panes as I did the inside.

My duties included picking berries in the garden for pies and jam—Mam always used me for this, too, since I preferred apples and wasn't likely to gobble up half a bushel before I got home, the way the boys would. That I was now getting paid to do what I normally did for nothing was exciting for me. I earned ten shillings a week, the equivalent of $2.80, which seemed like a fortune. Sometimes I would stop at the butcher shop on my way home to buy bacon, sausages, and maybe a scrap of meat to surprise my family for dinner. I would mix it all together with some vegetables to cook over the fire for a fry. What a treat that was! Putting together the occasional fry for everyone made me feel important and grown-up, and everyone, even Dad, would be in the happiest of moods. He even promised to help me shop for the bike I was saving up to buy. A cherry red one with skinny wheels, that's what I wanted.

The closest I'd ever come to having a bike was one my brothers and sisters and I had pulled from a heap of junk in the farm's storage shed. It had no pedals, no brakes, and no tires on the rims, but we would haul it to the top of a steep hill, start running, and jump on. Since there was no stopping the thing, you had to crash-land it in tall grass at the bottom of the hill. We had just as much fun with an old baby carriage we found. It only had two wheels, but that was all we needed to turn it into a wheelbarrow and push each other around. With no television to watch and just a crackly radio whose battery had to be charged in town once a week (it took three days, and Dad insisted on saving the battery life for his football matches the rest of the time), we had no choice but to make our own entertainment.

My favorite pastime of all, though, was playing camogie. Camogie was the most popular female sport in Ireland, a Gaelic game akin to hurling or field hockey. Both Briege and I were avid players—I was center-halfback—and it was a bright spot in our week to spend time laughing and just hanging out with other young girls, enjoying our game and even traveling to different towns for matches. If we went far enough away, the team would get a free dinner thrown in. Rose O'Rourke played, too. At twenty-four, Rose was by far the oldest one on our team, and not such a great player, truth be told, but her family's status in the county had cinched her the title of team captain. It was the only time I saw Rose act the least bit uppity. The camogie team was getting new uniforms, and Mrs. O'Rourke was making them for all fifteen players in the huge drawing room where she had her sewing machine set up. I stole a sneak peek at the yards of material she was cutting from her patterns—our skirts were a beautiful pale lavender with white sashes to match our blouses. I could hardly wait as the first game of our season approached. Rose began handing out the new uniforms but fell four short. Briege and I were among those left empty-handed. I would have shrugged it off and waited—I knew Mrs. O'Rourke was still working on the last of the uniforms—but Briege angrily confronted Rose.

"I don't understand," Briege railed. "My sister works for you, and you left us out?"

"You'll get your uniforms," Rose tried to assure her, but Briege was in high dander by then, suspecting Rose was engaged in some sabotage so we would be forced to sit on the bench—Rose's customary spot—in the opening game, leaving the coach no choice but to start with her. The rules stipulated that you couldn't play unless you were in uniform. We had never been substitutes before, and Briege was so indignant she likely would've rather played naked than be one now. Finally the coach stepped in, instructing two girls of similar size to give Briege and me their uniforms so we could be played in the match. They obliged, but for weeks after, Briege kept pestering me every day when I came home from work, demanding to know if "our" uniforms were done yet. It drove a bit of a wedge between Rose and me at first, but we quickly moved past it and let my older sister stew in her own juices.

Despite her family's prosperity, Rose really didn't put on airs, and I enjoyed working with her. She was lighthearted and funny, and her good company made my day fly by. She even taught me how to make fresh cinnamon-and-sugar doughnuts from scratch, which I eagerly demonstrated back at home for my own family, turning into a one-person doughnut factory as my ravenous brothers devoured plate after plate for two hours straight. When we were left on our own in the O'Rourkes' kitchen, Rose would turn on the radio and we'd dance like crazy to the likes of Elvis, Chubby Checker, and Buddy Holly. Rock 'n' roll still felt new and exciting, such a far cry from the traditional Irish folk music we'd grown up hearing. As much fun as we had, it was obvious that Rose longed for something more meaningful than me pretending to be Connie Francis in her kitchen. She wanted someone to slow-dance with. Most of the other girls her age were courting, engaged, or already married, as were her four sisters, but Mrs. O'Rourke had all but sealed poor Rose's fate as an old maid, strictly forbidding her pretty daughter to see the one man she truly loved, a strapping young farmhand named Peter who worked for the O'Rourkes.

For a while, I was cast in the role of messenger in Rose's secret romance with Peter. Peter seemed like a great catch—hardworking, good-natured, and handsome—but character was not as important to Mrs. O'Rourke as breeding, and she put her foot down, telling Rose in no uncertain terms that a common laborer was "not good enough" for any daughter of hers. Rose and Peter were not so easily put off each other, though, and simply shifted gears to covert mode. They managed to exchange a few words each day when Mrs. O'Rourke was out of sight, sewing in her drawing room or baking bread back in the kitchen. Peter would casually happen through the yard on some fake errand while Rose was hanging out the window or if we were outside beating the rugs or hanging clothes on the line. Recruiting me as a go-between, Rose would later send word to Peter about where and when to meet her for a longer rendezvous.

I was an eager accomplice, but at fourteen, not a terribly reliable one. As far as I know, the only lovers' quarrel Peter and Rose ever had was my doing, though I never did confess. The drama unfolded when Rose sent me out one afternoon to tell Peter to meet her at seven o'clock under the bridge along the train tracks, a message I did, in fact, convey. What I neglected to do, however, was specify which bridge and which tracks, and Peter assumed quite naturally that Rose meant the ones running closest to the O'Rourke property. So Peter went and waited, but Rose never showed. Rose likewise went and waited, but not in the same spot, and she came home fuming. How dare Peter leave her there like that? The next day, Peter sauntered into the yard while Rose was hanging out the window, but she kept her back to him and uttered not a word. He attempted a couple more walk-bys later in the afternoon, but she refused to talk to him that whole day. This was an interesting new twist to the soap opera, and of course, I wanted to know what was going on.

"Rose, how come you didn't say hello to Peter?" I asked after the first snub.

"I'm mad at him," she declared. "I waited for him last night under the bridge at the tracks going into Carrickmacross, and he stood me up!"

"Aw, that's too bad," I commiserated, hoping my face didn't betray the pang of guilt I felt that my carelessness had botched things up. How had the bridge and Carrickmacross slipped my mind? I felt so important having someone already grown regard me as a friend. If I told Rose the truth, I feared, she would see me for the silly little girl I was and never speak to me again. Peter would just have to be nudged in the right direction to get things back to normal.

On my way home that evening, he anxiously waylaid me.

"Kathy," he implored, "what did Rose say today?"

"That you let her down," I answered gravely. Peter furrowed his brow, hurt and puzzled. I told him I had to hurry home, then skedaddled before he could start interrogating me in earnest. They patched things up soon enough, but then one of Rose's older brothers apparently caught sight of the lovebirds together one day, and tattled to Mr. O'Rourke, who promptly fired Peter. He went to work for a neighboring farmer, and he and Rose carried on their secret romance as best they could.

My own teenaged flirtations played out at the Friday-night mixers held across the county. Just getting to the dance required some fancy footwork for Briege and me and our girlfriends if we were venturing beyond our own nearby village. Our cousin Mary Kirk would be used as bait out on the road, hips, chest, and thumb all thrust out in what we collectively decided was the most fetching pose. Guys always told Mary she had fabulous legs, which puzzled me, since they were frankly on the chunky side. But Mary drank up the compliments, and her hemlines crept ever higher. She was a good sport about giving her waistbands still another roll if that's what it took to get us a ride, so with Mary in place, the rest of us would retreat behind some bushes to wait like anxious stage managers backstage on opening night. Inevitably some boy on his way to the same dance would drive by. As soon as one stopped to offer Mary a lift, the rest of us would scurry out from our hiding place and just pile into the car with her. We never had an ambushed driver order us to get back out: Picking up one girl and being carjacked by four or five more probably wasn't the worst thing that could happen to a teenaged boy. Actually, that was yet to come, at the dance itself.

Inside the shabby clubhouse, all the girls would line up along one wall and wait for the lads lined up on the opposite side to cross the wide floor and ask for a dance. I always said yes, but some of the girls were mean about it and would refuse a boy if he wasn't popular or good-looking enough, or they were pointedly waiting for a better prospect to approach. The poor rejected fellow would then have to turn around and make the humiliating walk through the dancing couples back to the boys' wall.

I wasn't pretty enough or a good enough dancer to get asked very often, but it was still fun to go to the dances just to socialize. I'd go on a date or two with different boys throughout my teen years, but no one really lit my fire, and in my eighteenth year, I started to wonder exactly when my Prince Charming was going to materialize. I'd been working at the O'Rourkes' for four years and was eager to get on with what I envisioned my "real" life would be: marrying a decent, preferably handsome man with the skills to be a good provider, then settling down in County Monaghan to raise children of our own under circumstances less challenging than I had known growing up. Mothering would be my life's work. I saw myself happily serving bacon and eggs for breakfast and roasts for dinner, buying clothes new from the shop, maybe even hiring—instead of being—a good local girl eager to earn a few shillings by helping out around the house. When my fantasies took flight, they always landed quickly and safely at that station marked "Pleasant."

"Grand" was not even in the realm of my imagination.

The letter from America came on its own, with an extraordinary offer beyond the yearly boxes we anticipated so much: a ticket. Uncle Pat and Aunt Rose were inviting Packy to come live with them in the Bronx and make a good life for himself in the United States. They would loan him the one-way airfare, and he could pay them back over time. Packy seemed more nervous than excited; he was living with Aunt Bridge and Uncle Teddy, running their farm for them, and he liked it just fine. Briege was beside herself with envy, but I understood Packy's uncertainty. Ireland was harsh, to be sure, but I loved it deeply and was proud to be Irish. Our generation was the least likely to emigrate since The Great Hunger of 1845 to 1852, when blight destroyed Ireland's potato crops and forced the mass exodus of one and a half million people trying to escape starvation and disease. It wasn't long before there were more people of Irish heritage living in New York City than in Dublin. But in 1962, there was no natural disaster to flee, no hell to escape.

Aunt Bridge lobbied hard for Packy to stay in Inniskeen: There was no way she could manage without Packy's help, and she loved him like the son she never had. "I'll never see you again!" she cried when he told her the news. If Packy stayed, she promised, the farm would be all his someday. She and Uncle Teddy may have been bank poor, but they were land rich, and

Packy took the deal. Dad was furious at his sister for meddling, and at his son for changing his mind. This was an embarrassment to him, and an insult to Uncle Pat.

"How can I tell my brother you're not going?" he thundered. Packy wouldn't budge, though, and Dad had no choice but to tell Uncle Pat he'd gotten cold feet. Mick didn't want to go to America, either: He had plans of his own to look for construction work in England.

"Send one of the girls, then, instead," Uncle Pat suggested.

"Only if you'll take them both," Dad countered.

"You're not taking my girls away from me!" Mam cried, but Dad would hear none of it. If Briege went by herself, he argued, then I would just end up marrying some farmer one field over and living this same life forever. It was the closest Dad ever came to saying he wanted us to have something better than he could provide, or a chance, at least, of finding it. Sending the both of us, he knew, would lessen our homesickness, since we were so close, and we could watch out for each other in such a big city so far from home. Uncle Pat generously agreed to front both of our airfares. Briege screamed for joy when we were given the news. I was quiet, not sure whether the butterflies in my stomach were from excitement or fear. We took the train to Dublin to start the paperwork. We would need passports, visas, health certificates. If everything went through without problem, we would be on our way to America sometime after the New Year. Mam was still distraught about us leaving, and deep down in a place that all of us knew and none of us ever acknowledged, I understood that the pain at Mam's very core wasn't about letting go of two daughters.

Because it was three of us that would be lost now.

Mary had been the youngest of us girls, and the prettiest. It was obvious to everyone, though only Aunt Bridge was blunt enough to say so out loud. It was probably because Mary most resembled her, with her dainty features and beautiful hair. Bridge's was blond, worn in a braid she kept wound atop her head and never let us comb. Mary's tumbled in red waves down her back. Not a dark rusty red, or carroty orange, either. Strawberry blond, like red sunlight. Mary had the personality to go with it, too, always dancing about like a fairy. She was a year and a half younger than I was, left behind with Jim and John when I went off to the school with the older bunch. Owney wasn't born yet.

One December day a week before my sixth birthday, Mam was fussing over a sick turkey. It had the pip, a disease named for the hiccupping sound the sick bird made. They died if it wasn't caught in time, and the only way farmers knew to cure it was to cut dandelion very fine and put it in their feed. Jim, the baby, was sleeping, and Mam had left Mary and John playing in the house for a few minutes to go out to the yard and try to get some of the dandelion mixture down the dying bird's gullet.

We'd just gotten one of our big care packages from America, and Mary went rooting around for a new dress to try on. There were never any small enough for her, but the ones intended for Briege and me were loose enough to billow out like Cinderella's ball gown when she twirled. That was most likely what she was doing in the kitchen that morning. We guessed but never knew for sure that three-year-old John started turning the hand crank on the wheel that would blow air through an attached bellows onto the kitchen fire. It was easy to spin, and he would have seen his big brothers doing it. It was their job to keep the fire going. Whatever it was that happened, the flame got too high, and Mary, too close. The oversized gown caught fire. Mary ran out of the house screaming, but she had already reached the hay shed by the time Mam got to her.

When the rest of us came home from school, Mary was lying very still in Mam's bed. I couldn't see the rest of her beneath the sheet, but I saw her ghostly face, covered with the white salve Mam had made with baking soda and water. Mam's blistered hands were white with it, too. Mary's hair was all burnt off.

The ambulance came and took my little sister to the hospital in Monaghan, but they couldn't do anything for her there, so they transported her to the bigger hospital in Dublin, where she died a day or two later. There was no money for a hearse to bring her home, so Dad placed her casket in the back of a neighbor's borrowed station wagon for the three-hour trip. There was a funeral Mass that I no longer remember, and Mary was buried in our family's cemetery plot, with a simple cross marking her grave. I don't remember Mam, or any of us, ever talking about her. It was just something we all understood must be kept inside.

December rushed past in a flurry of farewells as Briege and I got ready to leave on January 8, 1964, barely a month after my nineteenth birthday. The night before we left, the camogie team threw us a party and presented us each a trophy on a marble base. I packed it into my ancient secondhand suitcase, along with my prayer book and a glow-in-the-dark Christmas ornament Aunt Rose and Uncle Pat had sent one year, a holly wreath with a nativity scene in the center. We never did have a Christmas tree, but it had served as a night-light when I was growing up, and I was quite attached to it still.

On the way to the Dublin airport, I checked my passport and ticket again just to make sure this was real. (Only when I got the passport had I learned my given name was actually Catherine, not Kathleen—I was a changed person before I even boarded the plane.) My Irish Airlines ticket was stamped "ONE WAY" in bold letters, a reminder every time I looked at it that there would be no turning back. From an observation deck inside the airport, we could see other planes taking off, plumes of what looked like smoke trailing behind them. I nudged my sister in alarm. "Oh my God, Briege, we're in trouble, look how fast they're going!"

Our plane sported a green shamrock on the side, and I wasn't sure whether to be reassured or concerned that the national symbol for good luck served as the airline's logo. We boarded and I fastened my seat belt tight. The stewardess began giving instructions, telling us we'd find our life jackets under the seat. I dove down and began groping for it, thinking we were supposed to put them on and wear them until we landed again. "No, no, you eejit," Briege admonished me. "Not now. Only when we're crashing."

Then the plane was hurtling down the runway, everything rushing by sideways out the tiny window. The wheels lifted up with a loud whining noise and heavy jolt, and there I was, flying. Fear gave way to excitement. Higher and higher through the clouds we climbed, Ireland becoming just a green speck below, growing ever smaller until, too fast, it slipped away.

THREE

Inside the Bubble

The frozen half-smile the outside world saw in formal portraits and scores of magazine photographs of Jacqueline Kennedy never hinted at the girlish sense of humor I sometimes glimpsed in the privacy of her own world. Like my squeaky shoes, the unique circumstances of her life conspired to create some great slapstick comedy at times. Seeing Madam's delight in those ridiculous moments made me feel a kinship I had never expected to, as if I had slipped inside a bubble that had a secret bubble within that no one on the outside could see. More and more, it was starting to feel not so much that I had taken Provi's place there but that I was finding my own. It was during those silly, spontaneous moments with the family that I felt most myself.

Once on a winter break in Palm Beach, Madam and her sister, Lee, were basking by the pool one afternoon while John, Caroline, and their cousins Anthony and Tina played in the water. The boys would have been maybe five or six then, and the girls a few years older. The Radziwill governess, Bridget, and I were getting ready for a rare night off in town. When I first got to New York, I had spotted an ad in the paper for cosmetology school. I had always loved styling my friends' hair back home and experimenting with the latest fads, like using beer as setting lotion. Seeing that ad got me excited by the thought that I could maybe learn the trade by taking classes in the evenings and on my day off, and I immediately enrolled. I only made it to a couple of sessions before my overprotective Aunt Rose found out and put a stop to it, saying it was far too dangerous for a young woman to be riding the subways alone at night. I still enjoyed playing beauty parlor with willing friends and coworkers, though, and I had spent a few hours that afternoon in Florida setting, teasing, and styling Bridget's hair into a half-up, half-down beehive with a cute little flip at the ends.

We came out to the pool to show off the final result. Madam looked up from the paper she was reading to rave over the hairdo. Bridget spotted Anthony running along the side of the pool and went to intercept him and make him slow down, but she was standing too close to the edge and he was moving too fast, and she ended up getting accidentally pushed in.

"She can't swim!" Anthony yelled, even as a Secret Service agent appeared like Superman out of thin blue air and dove in— dark suit, shoes, tie, sunglasses, gun, and all—to pull out the flailing governess.

The elaborate hairdo I had constructed was now plastered down over Bridget's face. It looked like she was being smothered by a mad otter. Bridget was unharmed but wailing and sputtering Gaelic curses. On her chaise longue, Madam was hiding her face behind her newspaper, but I could see the paper shaking like mad and could tell she was struggling mightily not to laugh out loud. Such a perfect lady, she could even carry off a soundless guffaw.

Like New York City, she was a riddle to me, both less than I expected and far more than I imagined.

It was funny how the paparazzi could so easily capture her aura of mystery, yet her more beguiling ordinariness always eluded them. She took my breath away every time I saw her in one of her couture gowns and jewels, off to the Metropolitan Opera's annual gala or some other star-studded event. "You look beautiful, Madam," I always told her, meaning it every time. And every time her face would light up and she would smile, thanking me and giving me a little hug on her way out. But a different, even lovelier light came through when she was at home, in her favorite tee shirt or turtleneck, in those tender hours when she could just be a devoted mother or friend, unscrutinized by the world. I was touched whenever I saw her eating lunch in the kitchen with John while Caroline was at school, sweetly indulging his endless questions and listening with delight to his funny little stories. Every day, I knew I could find her at her desk, deep in thought as she wrote long letters or dashed off quick notes to people who—like her brother-in-law Bobby, or her dear friend Bunny Mellon—might well be living mere blocks away. She went through rolls and rolls of stamps, stashed in a white wicker basket at her feet. She hadn't been widowed even a year when I came to her, and though I hadn't known her before, it felt good to see these glimpses of contentment. To know that she was going to be all right.

She was a handsome woman, to be sure, but to tell the truth, if you didn't know who it was you were seeing, your jaw mightn't drop the way it would if, say, Elizabeth Taylor or Grace Kelly happened to glide past on the street.

What drew you in with Jacqueline Kennedy wasn't perfection; it was a presence. It wasn't how she looked, but how she was composed.

Small wonder that most of us who worked for her tried to imitate her, in our own clumsy ways. Provi initiated me into that club while we were relaxing in the little staff lounge after a long day's work during my very first week. We had begun to strike up the beginnings of what would prove to be a lifelong friendship of sorts, often prickly but as stubborn, in the end, as both of us. Madam's recent move from D.C. to N.Y. had turned Provi's own family life upside down as a single mother with two sons. The youngest, Gustavo, was just a few years older than Caroline, and had been left in the care of Provi's aging mother back in Washington while attending the private school whose tuition, Provi confided, the Kennedys had always paid. Madam also paid for Gustavo to fly to New York each weekend to see his mother, Provi added, but such generosity couldn't make up for what Gustavo was missing. It had been agreed that Provi would stay on for a couple of months to whip me into shape and make the transition as smooth as possible for Madam before returning to D.C. to rejoin her family and work in the offices of Robert F. Kennedy. "I need to get back home and take care of my son," she said, taking a deep drag from the cigarette she held in a slim plastic holder similar to the ones I'd seen Madam use when she lit up the occasional L&M in her private quarters. Provi tilted her small head back and to the side, pursing her lips to blow out a plume of smoke with a well-rehearsed air of boredom.

"Take one," she said, offering her pack.

"No, thanks, I don't smoke," I said.

"You should try it," she urged, tapping one out for me. I shrugged and put the cigarette to my lips and lit it, inhaling 'til my lungs started to sting. I exhaled slowly, enjoying the cool relief. This was fun! I felt terribly grown-up, and before that first cigarette burned down to ash, I had become an enthusiastic smoker. It wasn't a cheap habit, I soon learned, and my brand of choice was OPCs—Other People's Cigarettes. I also salvaged the stale or crumply ones I found in Madam's pocketbook or evening bag when she switched purses. Provi had told me Madam had to have a few fresh cigarettes tucked inside whenever she went out, along with her favorite lipstick, a small brush, and a couple of quarters in case she needed to make a phone call. (She never carried money. She would borrow a few dollars off the doorman if she needed to tip a cabdriver, then send one of us right back down to repay him.) Madam didn't smoke in public and rarely used the ones in her purse. I was certain she wouldn't want the ones I was saving, but I was too ashamed to just come right out and ask her, even though she occasionally borrowed a smoke off me in a pinch.

Smokes weren't all I intercepted. Toiletries, oh, were those ever the grand prize: I could hardly wait for Madam to run low of the special bath oil she got from France; it smelled heavenly, and there were always a few drops I could coax out of a discarded bottle if I added a little hot water before shaking it into my own tub. Even better than the dregs of Madam's bath oil were the final drops of her perfume. Her favorite was Joy, a French fragrance said to be the most expensive in the world because it took more than ten thousand jasmine flowers and over three hundred May roses to create a single ounce. It was up to me to monitor every product Madam used to ensure she never ran out of anything, whether it was a wand of mascara, a bottle of shampoo from her hairdresser, Mr. Kenneth, or a roll of breath mints. As soon as she got close to using up the bottle of Joy she always kept on her mother-of-pearl vanity table, I would order a replacement through Nancy Tuckerman, then recycle the empty for myself when the new one arrived. The heady scent lingered even when the vial was bone-dry empty, and I could scent my lingerie drawer with it.

Madam loved to surprise people with little gifts for no reason; she was always buying books to send off to friends she thought might enjoy them. Whenever I dropped by in later years to say hello with my small children in tow, she would always go search- ing through closets or drawers for some toy or trinket to give them. I had benefited from that same generous impulse many a time while I was living at 1040 and Madam decided to cull her collection of peignoirs or costume jewelry or scarves. "Kath, is this something you would wear?" she might ask, offering a choker of rhinestone flower buds or a silk designer scarf in tasteful ma- roon and beige plaid. Nancy Tuckerman even let me pass along some of John's and Caroline's castoffs to some struggling Irish relatives with a houseful of children. "Just make sure to remove any name tags sewn in them," she reminded me. (Caroline prob- ably would have paid me to get rid of the smocked pastel cotton dresses from England that her mother insisted she wear; she absolutely hated them.)

Though my duties didn't include minding the children every day, I quickly fell into entertaining and keeping an eye on them as I went about my business, particularly John, who wasn't in school yet. John was hyperactive and had been prescribed medication for it; we also had to keep him away from sugar as much as possible or he'd really start bouncing off the walls. It wasn't that he was destructive or bratty, but both his energy and curiosity were endless. He would get up before the rest of the household, then proceed to make a racket rolling his favorite wooden truck up and down the hallway until someone—me, generally—came out to shush him.

"Let's go make pancakes, Kat-Kat!" he would suggest, pulling me by the hand to the kitchen.

"John, we'll get in trouble," I protested. The cook hated to come in and find our mess.

"We'll tiptoe," John whispered. It was hard to say no to John or tell him he had to wait for Maud to get up to start his own busy day. If I didn't come out of my room to keep John company, he would barge in at 6:00 a.m., pretending he was looking for his dog. Shannon had discovered that I appreciated leftovers and was always willing to share the haul from my midnight raids, so he had wisely taken to sleeping under my bed. Officially he was considered John's dog, but Shannon belonged to whoever fed and walked him, and once I started doing that, there was no going back. He was a terrible beggar, and I could never refuse his plaintive gaze. He followed me everywhere.

"Kath, did you bring Shannon in here?" Madam would groan sleepily when I came to wake her some mornings. "I know you did, I can smell him!"

I usually grabbed the dog's leash and took him with me when I walked to the newsstand to get Madam's papers and magazines. (Tabloids were her guiltiest pleasure.) When John begged to go one morning, I went to ask his mother if it was okay. She was grateful for the favor but didn't think to tell Maud, who was still asleep and went searching high and low for John once she got up. Someone finally mentioned that I'd taken him out. Maud had worked herself into a fine lather by the time we sailed back through the door. The children were *her* charges, she upbraided me, and I was not to take them anywhere without *her* permission.

Maud's high-and-mighty tone got under my skin, and I was sorely tempted to point out that the only reason I was minding John in the first place was because she had been sleeping. But she was old enough to be my grandmother, I reminded myself, and this wasn't a battle worth fighting, since I had nothing at stake.

"Madam said I could," I simply told her.

"*I am the one you need to ask,*" Maud huffed. Like Provi, she had worked in the White House, where the family's personal staff had the added support of all the White House servants. I was Madam's personal assistant, though, not Maud's. When I initially arrived at 1040, Maud tried to tell me I had to make the children's beds and clean out Caroline's birdcage. I knew better, and also knew if I let myself be cowed by her from the get-go that it would only get worse and more of her chores would end up migrating onto my daily task list.

"No, I don't. I didn't come here to do that. That's not my job at all," I told her bluntly. "That's your job." She hadn't bargained on me showing any gumption. She scowled and turned her heel.

It was no secret among the help that Maud was nearing retirement, and Madam was just waiting for the right time, and the right replacement, to ease her out. Caring for John and Caroline as babies wasn't as physically exhausting as caring now for active kids of four and seven. Caroline could quietly amuse herself for hours at a time, but John was a boy in perpetual motion, and Maud was over sixty.

One afternoon soon after I started, I heard Caroline and John in their back hallway fighting about something. John loved to torment his sister by sneaking into her bedroom to let her parakeets out of their cage, or scatter her toys. She seemed to have gotten the better of him this time, though: I heard a door slam and Caroline's triumphant shout.

"You're not coming out now!" Next came the sound of someone banging on a door, and a rattling noise I couldn't place. The commotion carried on with no indication that the usually strict governess was stepping in, and I realized that Maud was likely napping through it all. I went to the children's wing to investigate. Caroline had retreated, and the red-carpeted hallway was empty. The racket was coming from John's bedroom, where I was horrified to see a sliding-chain lock fixed to the outside of the door. John was trapped on the inside, rattling to get out like a gorilla in a cage.

"Let me out! Let me out!" he cried. The chain only allowed the door to open a few inches. I could see John's little face peering through the gap.

"Kath? Can you let me out?" he pleaded.

I had seen the handyman working on the door a few days before but hadn't noticed that it was an outside lock he was installing. Maud had been supervising. Now that she was in her own room snoring away, I put two and two together: John no longer needed a nap, but Maud did. Problem was, John would never stay put when Maud tried to put him down to sleep for a couple of hours so she could do the same. He'd bounce right up and go pester the cook in the kitchen, or come ask me to play, or even slip off into some other room to explore and look for mischief without anyone knowing he was on the loose. That generally ended badly, though not always as dramatically as the time he found an old firecracker in a buffet drawer in the dining room and the explosion brought the Secret Service barreling into the apartment with guns drawn. The blast had shattered a big decorative platter and filled the room with smoke. John was nowhere to be seen, of course. Madam hurried to his room, where he was scared and crying, but thankfully unhurt. Maud obviously thought that locking John in his room was the only way to keep him contained while she took her customary snooze in her room just across the hall, but I couldn't believe she had done such a dangerous thing. I immediately slid the lock open, and John catapulted out. I hurried off to find his mother.

"Madam, I think you need to know about something," I began. "I just found John locked in his room. There's a chain on the outside of the door, and I'm worried it isn't safe. What if there was a fire?" My fear was genuine. I knew there was no fire escape in John's room. I knew where every fire escape was in that apartment.

A rare frown crossed Madam's face, and she immediately headed for her son's room as I followed her.

"Oh, we'll take care of that," she said firmly when I showed her what I was talking about. "Thank you for spotting this, Kathy. You were smart to come to me." Her irritation gave way to a sigh that sounded more sad than anything. "I know she's getting on in years and needs to rest," she lamented, "but I'm not sure what to do." I felt a surge of pride that she was confiding such a thing in me and had acknowledged my sound judgment. Like we were on the same level, adult to adult. For once I didn't feel like the awkward, uncertain girl among the grown-ups.

The handyman was back at the door with his screwdriver in a matter of minutes, dismantling the lock. Maud never had a clue that I was the tipster, and if there had been any reprimand, the rest of the staff never knew. I started making it a habit to scoop up John and take him to the park to play in the afternoon, or at least out for a walk with Shannon while Maud dozed. He was fun company, and I even started meeting other Irish girls my age at the playground, watching their own young charges.

Working for the Kennedys was my first—and only, it would turn out—experience in being part of a household staff, and if I'd been anything but Irish, I doubt I would've survived a week. But petty jealousies, deep grudges, and bitter feuds are practically cultural traditions where I come from. When you have a bunch of Irish together, we all want to be better than one another. We're clannish and driven. The feuds were ongoing and the alliances ever shifting at 1040. Being so young, I was presumed easy to manipulate, but my youth also made the others all the more determined to keep me in my place. I was such an awkward girl, it was natural to assume I wouldn't stick up for myself. But one advantage of being a middle child in a large family is learning how to blend back into the sidelines quickly so you never get blamed for the trouble, even if you stirred it up in the first place. I was the absolute queen of the poker face, and anything but innocent.

The kitchen was usually where the staff wars were played out—an ideal battleground, since Madam's quarters were on the opposite side of the apartment. The players and the issues would change around, but the motivation behind all the fights remained the same: Everyone wanted to be at the top of the ladder, and the only way to claim that spot or hold on to it was to put your boot in someone else's face. It didn't take long for me to land in the grumpy old cook's crosshairs.

"You know what happened to those pork chops?" she questioned me, peering into the fridge the day after Madam had hosted a dinner party. I didn't need an invitation to enjoy a dinner party. Dinner parties meant leftovers, and both Shannon and I knew exactly what had happened to the pork chops in question. When you start explaining or lying is when you get caught out, I reasoned. I'd rather be considered dumb and get the pork chop. I pretended I hadn't heard Bea and waltzed off to wash Madam's unmentionables. Bras, underwear, and panty hose had to be laundered by hand each day. Bea was onto me, and I needed some quiet time to contemplate my counteroffensive.

"You're drinking too much coffee, and it's too expensive," came Bea's next challenge. I hadn't asked for Taster's Choice, but having discovered it in the pantry, I sure did like it, and last I checked, we weren't in occupied France. Neither Madam nor Nancy Tuckerman had mentioned any coffee-rationing program. Madam herself preferred tea; the instant coffee was for the staff anyway.

"You're coming down a brand," Bea decreed. "I'm not buying that for you anymore."

Room and board was part of our compensation, and Bea didn't control everything that went into our mouths, even if she was preparing staff meals. If I wanted a cup of coffee, or to fix myself a sandwich for lunch, I was well within the commonly understood boundaries of acceptable behavior. Snitching leftovers was more of a gray area. But I figured the cook wasn't going to reheat them to serve again to Madam, and Bea wasn't my boss, so why not?

Bea ordered the groceries, though, and considered them hers to dole out. I was still packing on the weight, which put Bea on red alert. She started counting the Yodels and Hostess Cupcakes in the pantry, and concluded—not incorrectly—that John and Caroline didn't devour that many that quickly. When the groceries were delivered, Bea made a big show of putting the goodies into a separate bag and taking them to her room for safekeeping. "Keep your paws off these," she warned.

"Bea, I wouldn't eat it when you slept with it," I shot back in self-defense.

My brazen incursions into her territory didn't let up, though, and I felt safe in the assumption that it was just me and the mice in the pantry after-hours, with no witnesses to ever prove I was even in there. Late one night, I crept into the kitchen to forage around for a snack and bumped smack into a shadowy figure in the dark. Both of us shrieked.

"Oh, it's you!" Madam laughed with relief. "I was just looking for some ice cream!"

I was glad she had caught me on my way in instead of on my way out—at least I was empty-handed. I took the opportunity to change the subject so she wouldn't begin to wonder what I was doing there in the first place at that hour.

"Did you know we have a roach problem, Madam?" I said.

She looked like she didn't know what I meant. I wasn't sure whether it was my accent or her unfamiliarity with the world of vermin.

"Watch," I said. "You'll see them when I turn on the pantry light."

I opened the pantry door and flicked on the switch. Sure enough, several cockroaches skittered across the floor for cover. Madam recoiled in horror.

"How do we get rid of them?" she asked.

"Well, it's the cook's problem," I helpfully explained. "An exterminator should probably be called in."

"I see. That's a good idea. Will you tell Bea first thing tomorrow?"

"It'd be better if you did that in person, Madam," I demurred.

Bea wasn't the only one always on the lookout for ways to put me in my place. Madam had only moved into 1040 a few months before I was hired, but May, the waitress, had been there first and considered herself therefore closest to Madam. May was in her forties and was not at all pleased that a young upstart like me had just landed Provi's job as personal assistant, which afforded me more status and power in the servant pecking order. I spent most of my day in direct contact with Madam, which meant I picked up more about what was going on in the household than the kitchen staff did. I relished the chance to rub that in their faces now and then as payback for being dismissed so often for my youth. If I got Madam's suitcases down and put them on the guest room bed, everyone's antennae instantly went up: They knew that meant a trip was afoot, and that I would know when and where, since I did the packing. I always needed a decent head start on that, since every sleeve, pant leg, and pocket had to be stuffed with packing paper to minimize wrinkling.

As soon as the suitcases appeared, May would start following me around, fishing for information. Where was Madam going, when was she leaving, how long was she going to be gone? Was it a weekend of horseback riding at her country home in Peapack, New Jersey, or a week abroad to see her sister in London? It wasn't idle curiosity: The staff staying behind knew they'd have it easy for a while, and having exact dates gave the sneakier ones a chance to plan some unauthorized days off if they knew the coast was clear. Madam was hardly as naive as they thought, though, and would compile lists of extra chores that needed doing while she was away. She loved writing out instructions, making lists, and dashing off thoughtful little thank-you notes for a job well done, whether she was gushing over a particular soup the cook served at a luncheon or letting a florist know how beautiful she found a particular bouquet. If she had a pen in her hand, or a book, she didn't need anything else for hours. It was my job each morning to make the rounds handing out her directives to the rest of the staff.

"You'll know soon enough," I teased May whenever she badgered me about Madam's itinerary. She was putting me in a bad spot anyway: I was supposed to be discreet, not the town crier. Unlike Bea, May was sometimes nice, and we went back and forth between being almost-friends and sworn enemies. I would just get to liking her, though, and she'd go and find some new way to insult me, like telling the guy who delivered the dry cleaning that she'd go get the chamber maid for him. I was furious when I overheard that jab.

"May, who's the chamber maid?" I demanded.

"You are," she said dismissively.

"You're just a dishwasher, you old Irish biddy," I fired back.

We all spent a lot of time telling each other what we weren't. May had had it out with Maud Shaw, too. Since Madam ate with John when she was home, the governess decided at some point that she'd take advantage of the respite and take her meal in her room, and she asked May to bring her a tray. May didn't like Maud in the first place because she was British, and being treated like her personal servant added all kinds of insult to colonialist injury. May groused about not being room service but delivered the food anyway. It was when Maud left the dirty dishes outside her door that hell broke loose.

"That lazy bitch!" May seethed. "I brought the tray up, and she didn't bring it back! She just went to the park with the kids and left it there, expecting me to fetch it for her!"

May hated any extra work and was downright diabolical when it came to avoiding it. When Madam added two or three guests to a dinner party she was throwing one evening, May had a meltdown over the prospect of serving extra people. She spent the afternoon grumbling and complaining, then turned on the waterworks just before the guests were to arrive and went to Madam, wailing about how it was too much to ask her to do and she couldn't possibly manage. Fearing disaster, Madam came to find me.

"Kathy, I'm so sorry," she apologized, "but May is terribly upset, do you think you could help her serve tonight?"

I agreed because I felt trapped, but I suspected May had an ulterior motive.

"Next time this happens, don't go to Madam, go to the secretary and say you can't handle the job," I told her. "You're a phony. If you want more money, ask for more money."

One time, May and Bea were going at it as usual, with May insulting Bea's native Galway and calling Bea chubby after Bea had yet again set May up to look lazy as a waitress by not telling her when Madam's food was ready, so it would be half cold by the time May noticed the tray just sitting on the butcher-block island in the kitchen. I was on the sidelines enjoying the drama when May suddenly flung the mug of tea she'd been drinking at Bea, splashing her white uniform. Bea screamed, but it was May who went running to Madam, crying about how mean Bea was.

Madam summoned me after she'd heard the confusing sob story.

"Whose side should I be on?" she wondered.

"If I was you, I'd ignore it," I answered, pleased that she regarded me as her trustiest source. "They're picking at each other all the time. They'll work it out." She agreed, and I breathed a sigh of relief that I had been able to circumvent further investigation and possible turmoil back in the kitchen. Madam circled back a couple of days later to find out what had happened.

"How are they making out?" she asked.

"Not talking, but they'll make up," I reported. And they did. But the truce, as usual, lasted maybe a day, two at most.

With the assassination not yet a year behind her, Madam was still in widow's black when she went out, and more given to intimate gatherings of friends and family in her red-brocade dining room than big, splashy parties at home. I never saw her crying or outwardly morose, but she never had much of an appetite, and the toll of the horror she had survived was plain to see on her painfully thin frame. Family was never far away, and both her sister, Lee, and various Kennedy in-laws visited frequently. Lee had an apartment a few blocks away, as did Bobby and Ethel Kennedy. Jean Kennedy Smith lived within walking distance, too, and her sons, William and Stephen, were favorite playmates of John. Their Irish governess, Bridey Sullivan, quickly became my best friend, and we spent hours chatting together in Central Park while watching the boys.

Bobby Kennedy had established residency in New York after stepping down as attorney general to launch his 1964 bid to become the state's Democratic representative in the U.S. Senate.

The president's younger brother visited 1040 regularly, usually showing up once a week to have supper with the family. John and Caroline would run and fling themselves at their uncle as soon as he stepped inside the door, clamoring for his attention. Bobby would toss John into the air and catch him, then get down on the floor to play.

He wasn't imposing at all for such an important man, I thought. Very skinny and not broad shouldered like the president had been. The first time he saw me, he had asked my name and flashed a big smile when I told him. "We have a Kathleen in our family, too," he said, referring to his oldest daughter. With eight kids of his own under the age of thirteen, Bobby stepped easily into the role of surrogate father for John and Caroline, and they worshipped him. Madam clearly leaned on him, too. Threatening to tell Uncle Bobby about any misbehavior was like telling the kids Santa Claus was going to find out.

In addition to his Manhattan apartment, which was close to his campaign headquarters in Midtown, Bobby had leased a twenty-five-room hilltop mansion as a weekend retreat in Glen Cove, on the northern shore of Long Island. It was like having a private hotel, with a built-in swimming pool and lovely manicured lawns with plenty of room for the kids to blow off steam with their cousins. Madam liked Glen Cove for all the woodsy trails where she could go horseback riding, and she rented a modest weekend home near Bobby's, a one-level fieldstone house with a stream out back where I showed John how to make paper sailboats to race under a small bridge. A couple of weeks after hiring me, Madam decided to give me a test run as governess with a family weekend in the country. I looked forward to the break in my routine. I felt at ease around the children; they were lively but well behaved, though not to the point of being little robots. Madam was going out for the evening the day we arrived, and I would be on my own with John and Caroline for the first time. Maud Shaw had left me a long letter on a sheet torn from a yellow legal pad, outlining specific instructions for the children's care—to make sure they brushed their teeth, said their prayers, and were in bed by eight o'clock. John was supposed to have a baby aspirin every night, too, to help with his asthma. I had just started to read the governess's instructions when Caroline snatched the sheet of paper out of my hand.

"You don't need this!" she announced as she gleefully tore it up. I laughed. I secretly shared her sentiments anyway. It wasn't in me to be strict the way Maud was, and I liked letting the kids get away with murder when she wasn't around. To them, I was the fun teenaged babysitter, not a governess. That night, they stayed up well past their bedtime while I gave them piggyback rides, throwing them off giggling into the couch cushions. When I finally got them wound down enough to go to bed, I remembered John's aspirin and shook out a little pink tablet to give him. I put it down and went to fill a cup with water, not realizing the aspirin was chewable. When I turned back around, the tablet wasn't there.

"Where'd the aspirin go?" I asked, checking the countertop and the floor.

"It's gone," John told me.

"Where is it?"

"It's in my ear."

I knelt down and held his head to the side as he squirmed, peering inside his ear. The aspirin had sunk too deep inside for me to reach. I decided to have John lie down and press the ear with the aspirin against a pillow while Caroline and I took turns tapping his other ear in hopes of dislodging the tablet. No luck, though Caroline thought it was great fun and wanted to keep going. In a panic, I called Madam's sister-in-law Jean Kennedy Smith, who also had a house nearby.

"Don't worry," she told me. "It won't hurt him. Those tablets dissolve. It'll melt away."

Caroline wasn't worried so much about her little brother's well-being as she was about Maud Shaw's potential reaction.

"Don't tell her anything," she urged me. I didn't need any convincing on that front.

Once the children were down for the night, I thought I'd take advantage of my bit of private time by calling my Aunt Rose and Uncle Pat in the Bronx to tell them where I was. There was a phone in the pantry, and I dialed the number. It was just ringing when into the pantry strode one of the Secret Service agents. Jack Walsh was handsome and imposing; with his suit and his gun, he made me think of James Bond. I realized I was using the Secret Service's phone and immediately panicked. I thrust the receiver at Jack Walsh, who put it to his ear.

"Hello?" he said, sounding very authoritative.

"Hello?" I could hear Uncle Pat saying back.

"Who is this?" the Secret Service agent demanded.

"What do you mean who is this, who are *you*?" Uncle Pat barked back.

My uncle and the Secret Service agent proceeded to fight over who called who until Jack Walsh hung up, muttering about some idiot in the Bronx. I was mortified and didn't tell either what had happened.

If Walsh said anything about my phone fumble, or Mrs. Smith told her sister-in-law about the aspirin fiasco, it must not have alarmed Madam, because after Glen Cove, I was in charge of the children whenever Maud Shaw was off. Bobby won his Senate race that fall, and Madam kept her rental in Glen Cove, too. It was a great place for the kids to play with all their cousins on the weekend, and Madam enjoyed riding horses there. It was her solitary pursuit. Ethel was that way with sailing, and Joan Kennedy, Ted's wife, had the piano. On the surface, at least, Madam struck me as more like her brother-in-law than her sisters-in-law, though.

Bobby and Madam had similar flip sides. Both had magnetic personalities, but then you would come to find out they were actually shy by nature. They were big on being outdoors and loved their sports, especially the ones that called for self-discipline or personal strength. Bobby and Madam were the Kennedys you were most likely to spot swimming farthest out in the ocean, no matter how cold the water was or how strong the tide. They were probably the biggest bookworms, too. Bobby was famous for being able to quote classic verse off the top of his head, and it was Madam who knew the perfect line for him to cite from *Romeo and Juliet* when Bobby paid tribute to Jack as he accepted the nomination for senator that summer:

> *"When he shall die,*
> *Take him and cut him out in little stars,*
> *And he shall make the face of heaven so fine*
> *That all the world will be in love with night,*
> *And pay no worship to the garish sun."*

There was no denying that Madam and her brother-in-law were close. Loss is a terrible love. No matter how much sympathy you have, it's a kind of pain that can only be felt, not imagined. And when it happens in a swift, horrific instant, there is no such thing as healing. Tragedy leaves you with an open wound, not a scar. I never told Madam that I understood these things, or how, but I could see plain as day that this awful shared knowledge was what made the president's widow and younger brother care for each other the way they did.

Six months into my new job, the suitcases came down from Madam's closet shelf again. She and the children were going to summer at the Kennedy compound in Hyannis Port, on Cape Cod. The whole clan was gathering there. Madam told me to pack my things as well.

"You're part of the family now," she said, beaming.

I smiled and thanked her, proud to have such a stamp of approval but torn between my growing fondness for Madam and a restlessness that was taking root deep inside me. I knew I should feel grateful to be accepted and perhaps, on some level, even loved. But I was twenty years old, and security wasn't what I yearned for. The Kennedys were special people—brave and brilliant, loyal and kind—I knew that firsthand. Much as I genuinely enjoyed being with them and even serving them, though, I didn't want to belong to them. What I wanted was to know what it was like, someday, to belong to myself. I would never have that if I gave myself fully to them. Their embrace was too strong to break.

When Madam told me I was part of the family, I felt the first stirrings of quiet rebellion, and I heard a small inner voice issue a firm warning: *No, you're not.*

This was all only temporary, never intended as more than a brief and colorful detour from the road I was meant to travel. Being a round-the-clock servant was my livelihood, not my life. Once my wages were no longer needed to help back home, I could return to my beloved Ireland, where I pictured myself raising a family of my own and someday telling my grandchildren the story of this enchanted bubble that held me, for a spell, right in the heart of Camelot.

FOUR

Coming to America

Declaring the chicken was my first mistake as a new immigrant.

In a city full of foreigners, the Irish probably had it the easiest in New York. Maybe it was because so many Americans have Irish roots, or because Ireland is generally regarded through rose-colored glasses. People tend to light up when you say you're from Ireland, then put on their best imitation of a brogue to say something the real Irish never do, like "top of the mornin' to ye."

That wasn't the case with the Customs agent.

We weren't even through the arrival doors at the newly re-named John F. Kennedy International Airport, and already I was in trouble. One look at my paperwork, and uniformed officials had ushered me out of the passport inspection line and off to a separate room to be frisked and questioned.

It had been Dad's idea to kill a chicken and wrap it up to carry in my suitcase as a gift for Uncle Pat and Aunt Rose, and without a second thought, I had dutifully listed it on the Customs form the stewardess had given us to fill out before we landed in New York City. Now I found myself trying hard not to stare at the gold front tooth of the Customs agent demanding to know more about my international chicken-smuggling operation.

I had never seen such a tooth! He was also the first black man I had ever seen, and his accent—Caribbean, as I would later come to recognize—was a strange new music I found as enchant-ing as it was unintelligible. I felt my cheeks flush with embarrass-ment as I struggled to pluck and decipher the words from the melody of his voice. I knew I must look like the village idiot, fresh off the proverbial boat, with a befuddled look on my face and a chicken in my suitcase. It didn't help matters that I was half deaf from the plane's landing; my ears hadn't popped and everything came through muffled and distant, like I was trapped beneath the sea in a submarine.

"Is this a live chicken you're bringing in?" the gold-toothed man wanted to know.

I tried not to laugh out loud at the thought of a clucking hen sitting beside Briege and me all the way from Dublin, though it might have been more bearable than the nonstop sobbing of our neighbor, Madge, an Inniskeen girl who coincidentally happened to be leaving home to join relatives in New York the same day we were.

The chicken, I assured the official, was most definitely deceased. "And plucked," I added helpfully.

"Have the insides been removed?" he pressed.

"No," I admitted. I wasn't sure I liked the direction this was headed.

"If you can put the insides on the outside, you can have it," he decreed.

Gutting chickens had never been my job on the farm in Ireland, and I wasn't going to make it my job in the middle of the airport in America, either. Were they truly expecting me to just jam my hand up the raw chicken and yank out a fistful of giblets? No, thank you very much. So now what? Whenever trouble was afoot, my tried-and-true response was to flatly deny any culpability whatsoever and walk away as quickly as possible. That clearly wasn't an option now, and I was getting nervous. I had never traveled to a foreign country before and had no idea what all the rules were, or what repercussions there might be for would-be immigrants who broke them, regardless of whether it was on purpose or not.

Did this misunderstanding mean both the chicken and I would be turned around and sent straight back to Ireland? Briege, stuck waiting outside the room with the weepy neighbor girl, was shooting daggers at me for being such a bumpkin right off the bat. ("I wouldn't have listed the chicken in the first place" was the advice she loftily offered long after it might have done me any good.) My jet-lagged brain groped for a solution. Maybe I could sidestep an international incident by turning the chicken into a goodwill gesture.

"Would you like to have it?" I asked the gold-toothed man hopefully. Surely his wife would appreciate a delicious chicken to cook for supper. Some soup or a stew, maybe.

"No," the Customs agent said, staring at the offending bundle with distaste. "*I* do not want the chicken."

"I'll just leave it, then," I said. He shrugged and put the packet aside, destined, no doubt, for the trash bin. I was only too glad to surrender the troublesome bird and get on with my new life in America. Aunt Rose and Uncle Pat would surely be wondering what was taking us so long to get cleared, possibly fearing we had been found to be tubercular after all. Finally, Briege and I made it through the last set of doors to the arrivals area, where our cousin John stood with a sign reading SMITH GIRLS.

John wasn't all that much older than we were, but he had his own car—so it was true that everyone in America was rich—and I watched from my backseat window as New York City flicked by like the jerky frames of an old silent movie as we drove from Queens to the Bronx.

I couldn't wait to see Aunt Rose and Uncle Pat's home. Even the name of the street where they lived—The Grand Concourse—summoned visions of stately brick houses with long, tree-lined driveways along a picturesque promenade. So far, though, all I was seeing on the way from the airport were streets with numbers for names, and endless blocks of ugly buildings jammed up shoulder to shoulder like grimy dominoes. There were cars everywhere, weaving in and out far too fast and much too close. Horns blared, trucks wheezed, and shopkeepers, deliverymen, and even pedestrians shouted on the street without a lick of self-consciousness— Buy this! Hey watch where you're going! and cries of Taxi! Taxi! Taxi! on every corner. I had expected New York to be elegant, a sleek and shimmering metropolis, not this rude, barrel-chested behemoth of a city. New York was the very definition of mind-boggling.

It sucked me right in.

"Here we are," John said at last, slowing to a stop. My heart sank, and I tried to hide my disappointment. Our successful American relatives lived in just another ugly apartment building. There were no trees or driveways. There wasn't even an elevator.

We hiked up five floors to Uncle Pat and Aunt Rose's place, where Aunt Rose had a nice dinner and welcome cake waiting for us. "Take off your shoes and leave them at the door," she told us, handing Briege and me little cloth slippers from Chinatown to wear whenever we were inside. *What a strange custom*, I thought. In Ireland, we'd never dream of taking off our shoes to come inside, unless we wanted our feet to freeze on the concrete floor. Aunt Rose's floors were covered with pretty Oriental rugs, soft even through my new Chinese slippers. I immediately confessed to Uncle Pat that the gift my father had sent him didn't make it through Customs.

"Why'd he send me a chicken?" Uncle Pat wondered aloud. "You can get them cheaper here."

"Well, it was all he had to offer," I explained with an apologetic shrug. I never did have the heart to tell Dad his gift was neither given nor missed.

Even though he was grown and had a good job as a New York City policeman, cousin John still lived at home, as did his sister Babbsie, who was a year older than I was and attending college. The two other sisters, Patsy and Bea, were married. Briege and I would be sleeping on the pullout sofa in the living room until we landed jobs as live-ins for rich families. "It won't take long at all," Aunt Rose promised us. There was a high demand for Irish farm girls among Manhattan's society ladies: We spoke English, had a reputation for being hard workers, and, as devout Catholics, were generally considered "good" girls unlikely to steal the silver or get knocked up by the grocery boy.

After sleeping off our jet lag, Briege and I were eager to explore our new city. I was itching to go look at the famous stores, like Macy's. I only had about ten dollars to my name—enough for a skirt or dress, and maybe a pair of stockings—but the list of things I'd need to Americanize myself was longer than that and would have to wait until after I got my first paycheck. The young American women my age all looked so smart walking along the sidewalk in their pencil skirts and high heels, with purses to match. I felt like a dowdy overgrown schoolgirl by comparison. I wanted to wear cute new clothes and sit at the lunch counter in F. W. Woolworth, eating a triple-stack bacon, lettuce, and tomato sandwich, careful not to smear my frosted peach lipstick. First, of course, I'd have to pay back Uncle Pat for my $200 airfare, but there was no pressure, and I knew he would patiently wait as long as it took for me to whittle my debt away bit by bit.

Uncle Pat was my dad's brother, but he was a softer and jollier version. When Briege and I got up from the table to help with the dishes, Uncle Pat shooed us away. "No, no, this is my job," he cheerfully explained as he scraped off our plates and filled the kitchen sink with soapy water. His wife cooked, so he cleaned. Like Aunt Rose, Uncle Pat was affectionate and warm, instantly folding us into his close-knit family. Nieces and nephews always got the gentler side of Irish men, I knew. Dad was the same way: If any of our young cousins were out playing with us in the fields, Dad's usual gruffness would melt away and he would offer his nieces and nephews praise, attention, and extra pieces of bread we rarely if ever got as sons and daughters. I guess it had to do with having no expectations when the children aren't your own, which frees you of worries and disappointments as well. Uncle Pat and Aunt Rose's children had all done well for themselves, and I was eager to show my benefactors that they had been right to invest in me, too.

Before Briege and I buckled down to workaday life, Uncle Pat urged us to take a day off to go visit the Bronx Zoo. My sister and I honestly would have much preferred to go window-shopping, or to go into Manhattan to visit Times Square and the Empire State Building, but Uncle Pat was absolutely hell-bent on us going to the zoo. In his mind, it was the ultimate American experience, and we shouldn't waste another minute without enjoying it.

"It's the most famous zoo in the world! You won't believe it!" he boasted, ticking off the wild animals in the collection with enough pride that you would have thought he had captured all three thousand of them himself. Admission was free, but for twenty cents, you could ride a camel. Didn't we want to ride a camel? It was January, and bitterly cold outside. I did not, in fact, harbor any desire to ride a camel. I would much rather have tried on camel hair coats at Alexander's department store, but there was no refusing Uncle Pat. Briege and I obediently boarded the bus he instructed us to take, and off we went to the zoo. We'd never been to a zoo before, but it struck me as more of a fair-weather thing to do. Clearly everyone else in New York City thought so, too, because Briege and I pretty much had the sprawling place to ourselves. We shivered our way as quickly as possible from animal to animal. The ones with caves or dens were wisely taking shelter from the cold—or even hibernating—but the monkeys were out and about in their big cage, and we paused to watch them play on the ledges and tree branches. I noticed a large male sitting close to the bars, literally just a few feet away from me, carefully peeling a banana. I observed him, fascinated.

"Briege, look, he's opening that banana just like a human!" I exclaimed. The monkey scampered up a nearby branch and re-sumed working on the banana. I took a step closer, gaping up at the monkey as he began eating. He noticed me watching him, and our eyes locked. I couldn't believe how humanlike his expres-sion was; it was as if we were having a silent conversation. Ba-nana still in one hand, eyes still trained on me, the monkey then reached down, grabbed his penis, and sprayed me with urine. I jumped back in horror while Briege wrinkled her nose and guf-fawed. I declared our day at the zoo over, and we headed back home. Luckily, the noses of New Yorkers are bombarded by so many city smells every day that no one on the bus seemed to no-tice the wafts of monkey pee coming off me. When we recounted our zoo misadventure to Uncle Pat, he immediately took the monkey's side.

"You threatened his territory," he informed me. Our eye-lock didn't signal the creature kinship I thought it had—it warned the hungry monkey that not only was I bigger but I was aggressive, too, and was intending to snatch his banana away unless he took defensive action immediately.

At least you didn't piss off the ape, I consoled myself.

Sightseeing accomplished, Aunt Rose took Briege and me into Manhattan the next morning to sign up at the employment agency. A steep stairway led us from the sidewalk to the subway station below, and Aunt Rose showed us how to use our fifteen-cent tokens to get to the platform, where throngs of people already were waiting for the next train to pull in. "Always stand behind the yellow line," Aunt Rose cautioned, pointing to the stripe painted inches from the edge of the platform, "and try to get a car that's not too crowded. Be sure your pocketbook is always closed and hold it tight against you." Death, molestation, and robbery were not options I was used to considering daily when I needed to get from point A to point B, but the giddy excitement of being in New York was enough to tamp down the sheer terror of it.

A long train rattled up, the swaying bodies and bored faces inside jerking to a sudden stop before the doors opened and people poured out. We nudged our way to some empty seats and took off. The train was scary fast, but my ears still hadn't fully recovered from the plane, so at least I was spared the full-volume noise of the subway system. Being underground, with the world's biggest city above me, was unsettling, like I'd been swallowed by Jonah's biblical whale. We were spit out on Lexington Avenue, where Aunt Rose marched us to Johnson's Employment Agency, which specialized in placing domestics with wealthy clients. The girl at the front desk had us fill out a questionnaire before conducting a brief, friendly interview.

"Do you have any references?" she wanted to know.

"No," I admitted. I had checked the box on the questionnaire saying I was interested in taking care of children. Briege was looking for a position as a waitress, figuring that serving a family's meals and helping at dinner parties would give her more free time.

"Most people like Irish girls, especially for taking care of kids," the interviewer assured me. Not having references was unlikely to be an issue. Proving her point, she picked up the telephone and dialed a number.

"I have a nice Irish girl for you," I heard her tell the person on the other end. "Can you see her in half an hour?"

She hung up and gave me an address on Park Avenue, then

made a similar call on behalf of Briege and produced a second address. They were only a few blocks apart, she told us. Aunt Rose got us there in no time and came inside with me to meet my prospective employer.

Mrs. C was an attractive divorcée who wore her jet-black hair teased high and shellacked into a fashionable flip that was so stiff I couldn't help but wonder if her head ever actually touched the pillow when she slept. She smiled at me sweetly and explained that her two little boys would be home soon. Paul was in the third grade, and Scotty was in the first. Taking care of them six days a week would be my main job, but when they weren't around, I would be expected to help out around the house, doing some laundry, making the beds, and running errands for Mrs. C. "You'll be very happy here," she promised. I would earn sixty-five dollars a week, with every Thursday off.

The apartment was quite pretty, with spacious rooms and plenty of light. My quarters were the sole exception. Located just off the kitchen, my bedroom was barely big enough for the single bed and nightstand it held, and the lack of any window added to my suspicions that it was probably originally meant to be a pantry or maybe a utility room. But there was a bedside lamp and a bathroom for me to use with hot running water, so I was already light-years ahead of what I'd left behind in Ireland. I agreed to move in the next day.

Paul and Scotty turned out to be as promised, sweet and well behaved. I walked them to school in the morning then busied myself with chores until it was time to fetch them back home again. I ate dinner at the table with the children and their mother but felt too awkward and self-conscious to appreciate what was supposed to be considered a privilege. I didn't like Mrs. C seeing how much I ate, or how rough my manners were compared to the Park Avenue etiquette even her little boys so effortlessly carried off. My fork and knife scraped and clattered across the china plates as I devoured every tasty morsel in front of me, occasionally stealing glances at Mrs. C as she soundlessly rested her silver between delicate bites and paused to dab the corners of her mouth now and then at crumbs that were never there. Conversation centered round the children and what they had done that day in school or with their playmates.

Once we were done eating, an automatic dishwasher cleaned and dried the dishes, though I really wouldn't have minded doing them myself the old-fashioned way by hand, just to kill some time before I had to retire to my nun's cell of a room, where there was absolutely nothing to do. I was still a teenager, after all. Beatlemania was sweeping America, but I didn't even have a little radio to listen to. How I missed my afternoons spent laughing and dancing with Rose O'Rourke as we did housework together! I wondered if she and Peter were still managing to sneak off together, or whether the camogie team had replaced Briege and me yet. Back home, I had always been the fun-loving one, and my

Park Avenue isolation felt almost physical, a heaviness dragging me down with a swift force, like quicksand. New York was thrilling on the outside, but inside, I was starting to fear that I had made a mistake that couldn't easily be undone. How was I supposed to make new friends? I didn't have a clue where or how to even begin. Everyone I knew in Ireland, I had grown up knowing. I couldn't even connect with my sister. Briege was living in her own cramped servants' quarters mere blocks away, but I felt too uncertain yet of Manhattan's screeching maze of streets to try to find her address.

A month after I began working for Mrs. C, I learned that the Beatles were actually going to be in New York—within walking distance, no less! Launching their world tour, the band was coming to perform on *The Ed Sullivan Show*. When they arrived at JFK, girls my age were screaming, swooning, and throwing candy kisses at them as they cleared Customs. I was dying to see them. Ringo was the cutest, I thought. I approached Mrs. C and meekly asked if I might take a couple of hours off to go and try to catch a glimpse of them outside the stage door at the CBS studio. I was so shy and unassertive, it had taken me all the moxie I could muster just to pose the request. Even if she wasn't part of the younger generation, surely Mrs. C knew how famous the Beatles were, I thought, and would understand that this was a once-in-a-lifetime opportunity! Even if the boys only appeared for a few seconds—even if I couldn't see Ringo and had to settle for

George!—just to say I was there would be worth it. My mind raced ahead while I waited for Mrs. C's blessing: What should I wear? Would I have time to fix my hair? Would Briege be able to get off, too?

Mrs. C looked at me with utter disdain.

"You're not going anywhere," she said.

My heart sank. I've never been a crier, but I felt my cheeks flush with shame, as if I had overstepped some invisible boundary between servant and employer. This was new territory for me, and not knowing for certain where my place was, I generally operated under the assumption that I had none at all, that everything beyond work was a favor. I had no choice but to accept Mrs. C's callous decision. And not only would I not see the Beatles in person, but I also wouldn't even get to count myself among the record seventy-three million viewers to watch the group's American debut on TV: Mrs. C wasn't about to invite me to come sit on the living room sofa and watch *The Ed Sullivan Show* with her, assuming she even tuned in herself for the historic performance. Her whole personality had proven to be a far cry from the sweet, welcoming woman who had hired me at first sight.

Cheery as Mrs. C had seemed at first, I quickly learned that her divorce was still fresh, and beneath her carefully shellacked surface, there simmered a tightly contained fury. My inexperience soon tested her boiling point. True, I had worked for the O'Rourkes for a good five years back home, but the way things were done there was familiar to me, and while considered well-off by Inniskeen standards, an Irish mill owner's home was a far cry from the class of Park Avenue. Even the cocktails Mrs. C fixed herself each evening demanded my attention and respect. Mrs. C displayed her liquor on the bar in heavy crystal decanters that required regular dusting. The decanters all had little chain collars that attached to the stoppers with tiny chain leashes.

"Kathleen, these chains are looking tarnished," Mrs. C observed one evening as she poured her gin. "Could you please polish them when you have a chance?"

While she was out the next day, I found the silver polish and started in on the absurd task, choosing a large bourbon decanter first. I hooked my fingers under the collar and dangled the bottle as I carried it to the pantry. Of course, the decanter slipped its leash and crashed to the ceramic floor, shattering into a million sparkling pieces. Guiltily, I quickly swept up the incriminating evidence and threw the shards in the trash bin outside, then sopped up the 100-proof puddle with a rag and got rid of that as well. It was a couple of days before Mrs. C noticed anything amiss.

"Kathleen, where is that big decanter?" she asked.

"I don't know, ma'am," I answered, willing my face into what I hoped was a blank expression.

"You're telling me you don't know about it, that you didn't see it." It was more a statement than a question, and her pursed lips told me Mrs. C wasn't buying my story. I walked away without answering, but thirty dollars was docked from my next paycheck.

I had discovered the first time I was asked to help her with the grocery shopping that Mrs. C kept a running ledger in her mind that was every bit as detailed and thorough as Sam Paugh's annual accounting had been with the farmers of Inniskeen: Trotting alongside her as she made her way down one aisle and up the next at Gristedes, my eyes had nearly popped out of my head over the selection of items to be had in an American supermarket. The deli counter alone was as close to a miracle as I'd ever seen. Mrs. C had casually filled her basket with meats sliced by the pound, then tossed in a fat jar of what looked like thick white custard, then a slim loaf of bread wrapped up like a birthday present in cellophane with bright red, yellow, and blue polka dots. "If you need anything, just put it in the cart," Mrs. C generously offered. I backtracked to the aisle where I'd spotted beauty products and scooped up some nice shampoo and hair conditioner, plus some deodorant that promised to make me daisy fresh.

Shopping done, Mrs. C pointed her cart to the checkout lanes and I began unloading everything on the moving belt. As my toiletries got closer to the register, Mrs. C briskly moved them to the end of the line, putting a plastic divider between her items and mine.

"That's yours," she had announced. It was a costly misunderstanding: silky American hair and perspiration that smelled like a spring meadow took a painful bite out of my modest paycheck.

Back home, we fixed sandwiches for lunch. I watched Mrs. C slather some of the white custard—a spread called mayonnaise, I learned—onto slices of the polka-dot-packaged bread, along with a perfect circle of pressed pink meat she had bought at the store's deli counter. I had no idea what animal baloney came from, but I loved it and it immediately became my staple—much better than the peanut butter and jelly that seemed to be America's most beloved national dish. I hated the thick stickiness of the peanut butter, and the smooth wet blob of jelly bore no resemblance at all to the farmhouse preserves of my childhood. Oh, but that bread! Even better than the baloney and the delicious mayonnaise. Wonder Bread. I could see how it got that name. Soft as a cloud. I wanted to cram the entire loaf in my mouth at once, which, given how airy the bread was, would have been easy enough to accomplish. "Put it away in the bread box, not the fridge," Mrs. C instructed me when we finished lunch.

That night, bored and lonely in my room, I waited until the house was deep in slumber, then crept out to the kitchen and took the Wonder Bread from the pantry. Opening the fridge as slowly and quietly as possible, I retrieved the jar of mayonnaise, then pulled a butter knife from the drawer of cutlery and stole back to my room. I sat on my bed and pulled out a slice of snowy white bread, then liberally smeared it with mayo and took a delicious bite. I loved the way the Wonder Bread collapsed between my teeth like an airy meringue, and the cold tangy-sweetness of the mayonnaise was like nothing I'd ever tasted before. One sandwich soon gave way to another, then another, until the whole loaf was gone. I tiptoed back out to the kitchen to return the seriously depleted mayonnaise jar to the fridge, and buried the empty polka-dot wrapper at the bottom of the kitchen trash bin.

The next morning, Mrs. C went to make her sons their sandwiches to take to school.

"Kathleen, where did you put the bread?"

"What bread?" I asked.

"The bread we got yesterday," Mrs. C snapped. What kind of stupid cow was I?

"I don't remember us buying any bread." I didn't lie unless I was scared or ashamed, but once I did, I was fully committed, figuring the penance was going to be the same at confession anyway. Besides, the church promised God's forgiveness but carried no similar guarantee covering Mrs. C.

"I know we bought a loaf," she pressed. "I told you to put it in the bread box instead of the fridge, remember?"

By then I had scurried out of the room while her back was turned, so my lack of an answer couldn't be taken as an admission of guilt. Mrs. C gave up and went out to run her errands, bearing a whole new loaf of Wonder Bread when she returned.

That day as I went about my duties, all I could think about was when I could get my hands on it. I figured I'd best wait a little while to deflect suspicion, maybe make the boys a couple of peanut butter and jelly sandwiches so a few pilfered slices of bread wouldn't be missed from the fresh loaf. The amount of time and energy I spent plotting my next raid only heightened my anticipation. I didn't just fancy this new midnight snack: I was craving it in the worst way.

At last I understood old Aunt Bridge's secret desperation when she used to send me to the shop to buy an ounce of pipe tobacco, claiming it was for my father to thank him for some chores, only Dad never saw it. I didn't discover what was really happening to the tobacco until I popped in unexpectedly one evening to borrow a bit of sugar my mother needed. Aunt Bridge was sitting with Uncle Teddy by the fire, and was curiously flustered when I walked in. I noticed a thin wisp of smoke curling up from her pocket.

"Aunt Bridge, I think your skirt is on fire!" I cried.

"No it's not, you cheeky little brat, now get out of here and go back home!" she hollered back at me.

Years later when I was grown and Aunt Bridge was old and sick in the hospital, I went to visit her and she gasped out a request for me to go to the gift shop and buy some cigarettes. My sister turned and looked at me with concern. Was Aunt Bridge's mind slipping?

"But she doesn't smoke," my sister protested when I headed for the door.

"It's for the nurses who've been so nice to me," Aunt Bridge quickly interjected.

I brought her the cigarettes and handed them over without an interrogation or lecture. In terms of guilty indulgences, I now reasoned, Wonder Bread with mayo was harmless by comparison. As soon as the house was sleeping that night, I snuck into the pantry. I did it again the next night and the next, too. It became an almost daily ritual. Mrs. C didn't say anything about her mounting Wonder Bread bill or my thickening waistline. She had bigger things to blame me for anyway, like what happened to the children's new snowsuits. The outfits looked like something an Olympic skier might wear, only in miniature: poufy jumpsuits in a deep navy blue, the attached hoods lined with fur. As I plopped them in the washing machine and poured in the detergent, I imagined how warm and cozy Scotty and Paul would be in them when we went sledding in Central Park, or maybe ice-skating on the big public rink there. When I pulled the snowsuits out of the wash, the dark navy blue was covered with big, mottled white splotches. The fur hood looked like a small, drowned hyena.

"What on earth did you do now?" Mrs. C demanded. "Good God, don't tell me you washed these in bleach? These were very expensive!" There went another big chunk of my paycheck . . . and another midnight loaf of Wonder Bread.

Wrath wasn't the only thing Mrs. C put on regular display, though.

The very first day I was there, I was lost in my own thoughts, picking up the children's toys or dusting or doing some other mindless task, when Mrs. C strolled into the room, casual as you please, stark naked. Not a stitch of clothing, and not a hint of embarrassment. She wasn't surprised to see me and just carried about doing whatever she was doing—she could've been sorting the mail or juggling tangerines, I was too shocked to take note— while I stood there horrified. I couldn't help but stare: I had never seen a naked person before, save for myself. Not even my own mother or sister. And Mrs. C was an alarming sight to behold, believe you me. The musical *Hair* may have still been four years away from hitting Broadway, but that woman was a walking billboard already. And this was no accidental flashing, either: Every single day she would go strutting through the house in the nude, even around her boys, who, at ages six and eight, didn't need that eyeful any more than I did. I felt sorry for them—no wonder they never brought playmates home after school for cookies and milk.

In the evening, Mrs. C often went out on dates, but there didn't seem to be any regular suitor, and the man she seemed most keenly interested in was her ex-husband. The first time he came around to pick up the boys for a visit, she insisted that I go with them.

"You don't have to come," Mr. C protested as I followed the boys out the door.

"She said I have to," I explained sheepishly. I was embarrassed and prayed he wouldn't put up a fuss. Mr. C furrowed his brow and shrugged with resignation.

"All right," he agreed. He would never be mistaken for handsome—he was short and balding, and wore big black orthopedic shoes that did little to correct his outturned feet. The poor man duckwalked like Groucho Marx. But Mr. C was a gentleman, and instead of resenting my intrusion on the limited time he got with his children, he gallantly included me. When he took Scotty and Paul out to eat, I was invited to come, too, and order whatever I liked—Mr. C's treat, and it wouldn't be coming out of my paycheck. I felt very out of place, and he had every right to feel annoyed, but he never let it show to me or the boys. When we came home, though, Mrs. C fell on me like a hawk, talons first.

"Where did he take you?" she wanted to know. Did I go to his house, was anyone else there? I gave vague nonanswers. "We went out to eat," I answered dutifully.

"What restaurant did you go to?" she demanded.

I told her we'd grabbed some burgers at a fast-food place.

"That cheap bastard," Mrs. C snorted. Her little boys traded anxious looks, and I knew they were desperately hoping I might speak up to defend their beleaguered dad.

"It's where the boys wanted to go," I said meekly, hoping the dirty look she shot me was the worst I'd get of Mrs. C's ire. Exasperation was her general response to my sorry existence, and now my shortcomings as a spy were about to send her straight over the edge. I was responsible for the boys, she tartly reminded me, and I needed to pay better attention.

Sure enough, I was foisted on Mr. C every time he came for the kids. Divorce was illegal in Ireland, the mere word taboo, and I was both curious and uneasy about being swept into such modern sacrilege. If my own parents had a grand love story, it was never one that was shared with or even glimpsed by us kids, but we understood that their partnership was unbreakable. We had seen it endure the kind of test no family should ever have to face. I wondered if Mr. and Mrs. C had ever actually loved each other, or just convinced themselves that they had until the fabric of their lie frayed and faded to the point that it became too weak to hold them and too thin to hide them.

Awkward as Mr. C's visits were, I began looking forward to them almost as eagerly as his boys did—it was like getting a little holiday, a chance to breathe easily and replace some of the oxygen Mrs. C sucked out of me. When the weather grew warm enough, Mr. C would take us out for weekends on his yacht in Long Island. Such a beautiful boat that was, so gleaming and clean; Mr. C let us have food aboard and never complained about the boys making a mess. I had my own cabin downstairs. Mrs. C always wanted to know after a yachting weekend whether any other woman had been on the boat, or went out to eat at a restaurant with us. But there never was. If Mr. C had a romantic life, he kept it private, and the time he had with his sons belonged solely to them—and the tagalong nanny, of course. He figured out early on that I wasn't in cahoots with his shrewish ex-wife, and Mr. C and I actually became friends, or at least formed the kind of un-spoken bond hostages do when they share a common oppressor. My role when I was with him was exactly the same as it was when I was with Mrs. C—the governess—yet Mr. C never made me feel stupid, or like a dull child who needed constant correction.

As summer rolled around, Mrs. C announced that I would be taking the boys to the house she had rented in the Hamptons while she stayed in the city. We were to spend our days poolside at her beach club, where we could eat both lunch and dinner, putting it on her running tab. A taxi would pick us up at ten o'clock each morning and bring us home at five. Did I have a swimsuit?

"No, ma'am," I answered. Ireland is wet enough as it is; swim-ming pools are about as common there as saunas in the Amazon. Coming to America, I had packed a Christmas ornament with a glow-in-the-dark baby Jesus and a raw chicken in my solitary suit-case, and even if I'd had more room, a swimsuit wouldn't have made the cut.

"We'll have to get you one," Mrs. C decided. Off we went to

a shop clearly meant for women Mrs. C's age, not mine. She pawed through the racks as I searched in vain for something even remotely my style or appropriate for someone of my generation.

"Here," Mrs. C said, holding out a hideous floral number with an old-lady skirt around the bottom.

"Oh, no, I don't think that will fit," I protested.

"Just try it on," Mrs. C insisted. This outing had been her idea, not mine, but already she was losing patience.

I went into the dressing room and pulled on the awful bathing suit. *Sports Illustrated* had published its first annual Swimsuit Issue just a couple of months earlier, with a gorgeous young model in a scandalous white bikini on the cover. Department stores and catalogs were full of cute two-piece suits in the bold patterns and neon colors heralding the "mod" look from London. I loved to window-shop with Briege as we put together our fantasy wardrobes full of Twiggy-inspired miniskirts and cute baby doll dresses. My fantasy self looked nothing like the dowdy matron staring back at me in the dressing room mirror. The flounce just added insult to injury. I wanted to burst into tears. I had put on more than forty pounds since coming to America—stress, boredom, and mayo–Wonder Bread sandwiches will do that to you—and I was going to look like a sack of potatoes no matter what I tried on. I was disgusted with myself and felt that I didn't deserve anything pretty, so I put up no protest when Mrs. C told the salesgirl to ring it up. And guess what? I had to pay for it, too. It wasn't anywhere near as cheap as it looked!

Even though I was putting in more hours for no extra pay, the Hamptons felt like a secret vacation. True, Mrs. C was never around, which made me in charge of the boys around the clock and all weekend, too, with no day off, but Scotty and Paul were fun company, and they never gave me a bit of trouble. I was more like a fun big sister than a babysitter. We ordered hot dogs and hamburgers at the pool for lunch every day, and ate dinner at the country club restaurant when we weren't down at the beach for one of the club's big sunset barbecues. No more weeping in my room over mayo sandwiches. A new indulgence soon replaced my Wonder Bread habit, though, thanks to the old farmer next door.

"Ever seen one of these?" he had asked me one day, hoisting what looked like an overinflated cucumber of sorts. I shook my head dubiously.

"It's a watermelon. You gotta try this," he urged, beckoning me to follow him inside. He set the mutant cucumber on the cutting board and split it open with a big knife, exposing the red fruit inside. I bit into the wedge he offered, then devoured it greedily. Heaven. I had just tasted heaven. Beaming, the neighbor gave me the rest of the melon and I took it home and went into Wonder Bread mode, eating the entire thing that day. My belly ached all night. I spent the rest of the season gorging on watermelon. Between all the sugary fruit, and the daily cheeseburgers with fries I ate while lazing around the pool all day, the calories piled up.

I'd left Ireland a lively, athletic girl with the kind of legs boys always noticed, and now here I was, hardly six months later, trapped not only in a lumpy body I no longer recognized but in a life I didn't like much more. Something was going to have to change, and soon.

Summer ended far too quickly, and being back under Mrs. C's thumb depressed me more than ever. On my Thursdays off, I would get out of the apartment as soon as possible, no matter what the weather. I'd wander the city and browse through all the shops until it was time for Briege and I to take the subway back up to the Bronx for our weekly dinner with Uncle Pat and Aunt Rose. How good it felt to be with family again, to just be myself for a few hours! Going back to Mrs. C's house filled me with a growing sense of despair. I was a hard worker, and a quick learner, but I was always being scolded for some blunder or other, and my self-esteem was running on empty. When Aunt Rose bought Easter outfits for Briege and me, I felt so pudgy and plain in my powder-blue suit with its old-biddy net hat that I flushed with humiliation when I heard my cousin and her boyfriend chuckling on the subway as we all headed to a nursing home to pay a holiday visit to an elderly auntie. "Are they laughing at us?" I whispered to Briege, who looked smart in her new navy blue suit. "Of course not!" she answered, thrown by the insecurity she could see growing deeper in me by the day. America was supposed to turn us from sheltered little farm girls into confident, modern young women. We were on life's superhighway now, but I seemed to have shifted dangerously into reverse.

Briege and I had saved up the money we didn't send back home to Ireland and pooled our meager savings to buy a small record player, which we shared back and forth, carting it across the Upper East Side. I remember one dreary Thursday when I had nowhere to go, and no one to spend the empty day with, and before I knew it, I had worked myself into the worst wave of homesickness I'd felt since leaving Ireland. I moped and wept my way up Park Avenue to see my sister, who was in the middle of serving a big dinner party. "What're you doing here?!" Briege exclaimed, bustling me down the hallway and shoving me unceremoniously into her tiny bedroom. She felt bad enough to check up on me a few times and smuggle me a leftover dessert as I wallowed in my misery. Flung across her narrow bed, I sniffled and sobbed with self-pity while I played my favorite song over and over again on the record player. "That's me," I wailed into the pillow as Kitty Wells sang sadly about "these four walls" closing in on her.

Briege knew I wasn't happy at Mrs. C's, but I didn't tell anyone, not even Aunt Rose, just how miserable I truly was. I did, however, let Aunt Rose know that my one day off a week kept getting shorter and shorter. "What do you mean?" she wanted to know. I explained Mrs. C's latest method of psychological torture: sleeping in on Thursday mornings. The whole day was supposed to be mine, but with her refusing to rouse herself and come out of her locked bedroom, I had no choice but to feed the boys and walk them to school. Once back at the apartment, I had to wait longer and longer for Mrs. C to come out of her room and give me my paycheck so I could leave. She knew I always took it straight to the bank. It was sometimes well into the afternoon before I could collect the money due me, race out of the apartment, and rush to the teller's cage to make my deposit before the bank closed at three o'clock.

"She's playing a game is what she's doing," Aunt Rose concluded. "You just need to beat her at it."

"And how am I supposed to do that?" I wondered. Aunt Rose merely smiled and said she was sure a clever girl like me would think of something.

The answer came to me like a gift from glow-in-the-dark baby Jesus. I didn't even have to wait long to launch my counterattack. Mrs. C's social calendar was nice and full that week.

"Kathleen, I'm expecting a gentleman to call around seven-thirty," she loftily informed me one afternoon. "Show him inside and tell him to make himself at home. Be sure to let me know as soon as he arrives." With that, she headed to her room to start the leisurely process of getting ready. I knew her routine well by then.

When the doorbell rang, I answered it promptly and greeted her date, showing him into the living room. I dutifully pointed out the bar and urged him to make himself a drink. Then I busied myself folding napkins in the dining room, where I could keep an eye on things. Soon enough, as if on cue, Mrs. C came striding out to make her cocktail.

Naked.

Too late, she spotted her visitor, shrieked, and streaked back down the hallway. I hightailed it to my room and laughed until my sides hurt. They still went on their date, Mrs. C no doubt giving her suitor an earful about her stupid Irish girl.

That Thursday, Mrs. C remained in her room as usual. I knew she was less likely than ever to make any effort that would allow me to get to the bank on time, much less to enjoy the full day that was supposed to belong to me alone. I came home from walking the boys to school and hurried to my room to change and gather my things. I always tried to be noisy about it, hoping Mrs. C would take the hint and come out. This time, I fairly stomped down the hallway to the front door, opened it, then shut it with a good bang. I tiptoed back to Mrs. C's bedroom and planted myself right outside her door, which she flung open a minute later. She was surprised to see me glowering at her.

"I thought I heard you leave," she blustered.

"Oh, no, not yet. I'd like my check now, please," I said firmly, looking her dead in the eye so she'd have no doubt who had won this battle of wits. She got her purse and wrote out my check.

It was the last time she tried to cheat me out of my day off.

＊

I'd been working for Mrs. C for almost ten months when Uncle Pat shared a bit of interesting news: A famous lady was looking for an Irish girl, and we had an inside track for the position, thanks to my cousin Patsy's husband, Jack, and the Irish police network. Briege was given first dibs, being the older sister, but she quickly declined: She liked where she was, and she preferred waitressing. This position was as a personal maid, with the possibility of some child care duties as well. I was happy to do two jobs to escape my one.

"It's Jacqueline Kennedy," Uncle Pat confided. "The president's widow."

When I got back to Mrs. C's after my interview that fateful Thursday and gave her my notice, our farewell scene was perfectly predictable: She ripped me up one side, and down the other.

"Who would hire *you*?" she demanded with a cruel laugh. "You ruin everything!"

"I'm going to work for Mrs. Jacqueline Kennedy," I informed

her. Her eyebrows shot up in surprise, but she wasn't about to lose momentum when she was on a mean streak.

"*Her?*" she shrieked. "Who'd work for that one? She's a *horrible* woman," she said, as if she played bridge with the most famous woman in the world every Tuesday and had naked cocktails with her on the weekend. "You're better off staying with me. You're making a big mistake. You're going to regret this."

I never did.

FIVE

Summers at the Cape

A Kennedy summer could begin only after you greeted Grandma Rose.

It was a ritual every family member followed religiously, so shortly after arriving at Hyannis Port that first glorious season by the sea, I went with John and Caroline as they bounded across the wide lawn to the biggest house in the cluster of white clapboards that make up the celebrated Kennedy compound. Atop a tall flagpole, an American flag snapped and furled in the salt breeze off Nantucket Sound, and I could see a passel of kids already playing down at the beach, their shouts and laughter floating up the hill.

Rose Kennedy was watching the same scene from a chair up on her broad porch, her weathered, patrician face hidden by a big sunhat and clip-on shades over her eyeglasses. Eager for the rare chance to have their grandmother to themselves without the competition of two dozen cousins, John and Caroline scampered up the steps. Rose glanced up from their hugs as I caught up to them.

"Oh, you're Jackie's girl," she said by way of introduction. It was friendly enough, and I took it as a welcome rather than a dismissal.

"Hello, yes, I'm Kathy," I introduced myself. My brogue was the only cue Rose needed to launch full steam ahead into a discourse about Ireland, half history lesson, half reflections from her visits to the country her own grandparents had emigrated from. They were Limerick people.

My name must've gotten lost somewhere in her reverie, because Rose never did use it in all the years she saw me. There were so many governesses, baby nurses, cooks, waitresses, and other staff members descending on the compound—nearly all of us Irish—that keeping names straight would have been vexing, for sure.

Besides, I decided that I liked my new moniker: *Jackie's girl.* It reminded all the rest of the help that I worked for the most special one.

Madam became a different person at the Cape, too.

Our house turned out to be the farthest back on the six-acre property, tucked on Irving Avenue behind Bobby and Ethel's sprawling place, which never was big enough to contain all the children, friends, help, and various guests who were forever spilling out of it. (Ethel even converted a big old playhouse in the garden into cute guest quarters at one point, and the running joke was if you parked your car outside Ethel's and left it unlocked, she'd have someone sleeping in it that night.) Madam's home was slightly more modest, not as close to the waterfront as the big house and Bobby and Ethel's, but with a stunning ocean view from a widow's walk that could be reached by squeezing up a little ladder hidden behind a door in Caroline's room. The Secret Service worked out of a trailer close by the gate nearest us—not that the round-the-clock presence of armed federal agents kept Grandma Rose from hectoring us daily about keeping the gate closed. ("Check again!" she would order when we assured her for the umpteenth time that yes, we had closed it, and we'd better be sure about it, because wouldn't you know she would march over to see for herself.)

Madam's house, I came to learn, was unchanged from the days when she and JFK had come to spend summers there as a young couple. But when he became president, the First Family moved to a nearby house on Squaw Island instead, for security reasons. Squaw Island, where Teddy and Joan Kennedy spent the summer, was more isolated, with only one road going to and from the narrow neck of land it was on.

A closet off the living room in the Irving Avenue house still held JFK's leather golf bag. On a shelf inside was an American flag, which John was in charge of carefully removing each morning to hoist up the flagpole in front of the house, then bring down again at sunset. Even at five, he knew exactly how to fold the flag back up again in triangles. "Don't let it touch the ground!" he warned me as I helped.

Madam hired a summer waitress and cook, and Provi was invited back to have a holiday with her son Gustavo. We settled happily into our new quarters and old feuds. I was thrilled when my recommendation helped land my cousin Babbsie a seasonal waitress job with Jean Kennedy Smith and her family. Shannon the spaniel came along for the summer, too, and made himself right at home under my bed as usual, which was fine by me until the evening he went out and got sprayed by a skunk.

"Oh my God, what is that smell?" Madam cried as he came running back inside. The two of us hustled him into the bathtub, me holding the wriggling dog down while Madam shampooed him, lathering him up again when the foul odor lingered, the both of us laughing and jumping away as Shannon shook himself, sending droplets of stinky water flying.

"What're we going to do with him?" Madam cried, still laughing.

A young Kathy in Inniskeen, Ireland.
Photo courtesy of author's collection

Taken on her first trip back to
Ireland, in 1966, after beginning
her job with Mrs. Kennedy,
a young Kathy went with her
sister to the spot they used to
go to each Easter Sunday.
Photo courtesy of author's collection

Kathy, back row center, at home in Inniskeen with her camogie
teammates at school. Her sister Briege is in the back row on
the far left.
Photo courtesy of author's collection

Kathy on a skiing trip with young John.
Photo courtesy of author's collection

John and a friend goofing off at bath time.
Photo courtesy of author's collection

Caroline with her grandfather,
Joseph Kennedy.
Photo courtesy of author's collection

John with his pail
exploring the dunes.
*Photo courtesy of author's
collection*

Young Caroline playing games with
friends at a ski lodge in Vail, Colorado.
Photo courtesy of author's collection

Kathy and John playing with Shannon on
the beach in Hyannis.
Photo courtesy of author's collection

Right: Jackie
and John in
Newport,
Rhode Island.
*Photo courtesy of
author's collection*

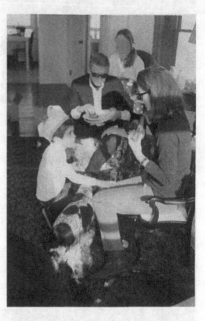

Above: Jackie, John, and Mike
Nichols eating lunch in Newport,
Rhode Island.
Photo courtesy of author's collection

Left: Jackie and
John riding their
show horses on
the Cape.
*Photo courtesy of
author's collection*

Above: Jackie and Aristotle
Onassis on the island of
Skorpios, Greece.
Photo courtesy of author's collection

Left: Jackie, Caroline, and Aristotle
Onassis.
Photo courtesy of author's collection

Kathy and another staff member
being silly in the hallway.
Photo courtesy of author's collection

Kathy and a coworker
in the governess's room in
Mrs. Kennedy's apartment.
Photo courtesy of author's collection

All dressed up and ready to leave
on a trip to Ireland.
Photo courtesy of author's collection

The Kennedy family at Kathy and Seamus's wedding.
Photo © John Twohig, courtesy of author's collection

Jackie admiring Kathy's ring at her wedding.
Photo © John Twohig, courtesy of author's collection

Notes to Kathy from Mrs. Kennedy that are among Kathy's most treasured possessions.
All photos on this page are courtesy of author's collection

Merry Christmas dearest
Kath
and much love from
us all
J.

April 1966

For Kathleen — a fan from Spain
affectionately
Jacqueline Kennedy

For dearest Kath
with all my happiest wishes
at Christmas —— and much love
Jacqueline Kennedy Onassis

much love at Christmas to
dear Kathleen and your
beautiful babies
Jacqueline Onassis

Merry Christmas to dearest
Kath —
You will certainly have a
Happy New Year!
much love Jacqueline Onassis

"Well, he's not coming to bed with me, that's for sure!" I answered.

The stench didn't go away even after John tied the dog to a tree and tried hosing him down. Shannon reeked for days. I let him out first thing in the morning so he could go visit his friend Freckles at Ethel's house and air out over there while stealing Freckles's breakfast. Shannon always got plumper in the summer because he'd go from house to house helping himself to all the other dogs' food. The Cape was an all-you-can-eat buffet as far as Shannon was concerned.

Attending to Madam's needs was light duty in Hyannis Port, but I was serving as governess as well. Maud Shaw had abruptly retired just before we left, after going home to England for her brother's funeral, and Madam wanted me to fill in as governess until a replacement could be hired. There was no extra pay to do so, but minding John and Caroline was easy at the compound, where everyone's help—plus the Secret Service—meant a collective eye was kept on the children as they ran around playing from house to house. There were bikes and golf carts to ride, playhouses, and all manner of sports equipment. The kids all loved being out on the water, swimming, surfing, sailing, fishing, waterskiing.

"We are tied to the ocean," President Kennedy had once been famously quoted as saying, and nothing at the Cape could be more obvious. John was the exception to that rule. Oh, he loved the water, too, but his true fascination was with airplanes. A small vintage plane was kept out on the lawn for the kids to climb around on—it was green, and maybe left over from World War II, I never knew—and John couldn't get enough of it. He loved to sit in the pilot's seat and fiddle with all the levers, making engine noises as he pretended to take off. The rest of the Kennedys may have felt the pull of the sea, but John always belonged to the sky.

Madam made sure the kids' days were packed with outdoor activities, including tennis, swimming, and water-skiing lessons. Caroline was always in a hurry to get started ("No, Caroline, you have to put the right clothes on for tennis," Madam would scold when she caught her trying yet again to pull her tennis shorts over her swimsuit.) The swim instructor, a local guy named Sandy, would also come by every afternoon at three o'clock to coach a baseball game with all the kids. Caroline was a tomboy who could hold her own with her competitive cousins, but John always had to be coaxed out of his room, where I would find him hiding out with his comic books.

"John, Sandy's looking for you," I would remind him when the baseball game was getting under way.

"I'm not feeling well," he often said. Truth be told, he *was* somewhat sickly as a little boy, prone to respiratory trouble, and he was slighter than most of the other boys in the extended family. They homed in on John as the runt of the litter and liked to pick on him the way big brothers do, seeing if they could make him cry. John didn't like rough-and-tumble sports and wasn't very good at them as a little guy, but between touch (more like slam) football, baseball games, and water polo matches that involved near-drownings, rough-and-tumble was how this family played. His mother didn't want him lollygagging around inside all day, and I knew from growing up with so many brothers myself that the only way to toughen up was to just keep throwing yourself back into the fray.

"Come on, it'll be fun," I wheedled John. I had never seen baseball until the Kennedys introduced me to it, but I quickly came to look forward to the raucous afternoon games as much as John dreaded them. They reminded me of my camogie matches back in Ireland. The governesses, waitresses, and other help cheering from the sidelines were always welcome to join the fun, and my best friend, Bridey, was a natural at it. Bridey could hit the ball like nobody's business, and she tore around the bases like a true Kennedy, with no apologies for plowing into or right over any adult, child, or excited dog in her way. I was still trying to figure out the game when she egged me on to take a turn at bat one afternoon.

I gripped the wooden club and took a wild swing as the ball came flying at me, surprised when I felt it connect with a solid, satisfying *thwack*. I stood there admiring my work: The ball flew high and fast over the heads of all the outfielders. "GO!!! GO!!!

GO!!!" everyone was yelling. I thought they meant the ones chasing after the ball.

"Wow, you know how to hit it!" Bridey said with admiration.

"Well, I know that part," I agreed. "But where do I go now?"

Bridey ran me around the bases, and I went down in summer history as the most clueless home run hitter ever. I always wanted to get in the game after that, but if John stayed upstairs, I was stuck inside, too. When he did come out, Sandy couldn't wait to come looking for Madam after the game. He was a little pushy and would walk straight through the kitchen toward the living room, where Madam could often be found writing letters on her blue seashell stationery or with her face buried in a book. Sandy would launch right in on a play-by-play of the game, making up stories of how good John was at it. "He made the bases," he would fib, when John had actually spent much of the game making up excuses about why he urgently needed to leave. (His leg hurt, or his stomach, or his toe—it didn't matter, because no one ever bought it anyway. The only part of dear, sweet John that wasn't Irish was his pitiful lack of imagination and commitment when it came to lying.)

Madam always listened politely to Sandy's fibs and thanked him for coming to play with the children. She would come watch the baseball games herself sometimes and knew full well that John was no Mickey Mantle in the making, but she just wanted him to get some fresh air and exercise was all, not a spot in the World Series.

Sandy had plenty of company when it came to locals wanting to weasel their way into Madam's good graces. Hyannis Port was a little summer beach town that depended on tourism, and the Kennedys were its biggest draw. It was money in the bank for any of the small shops or restaurants in town to boast of some connection to the family. People would send over baskets of goodies for Madam and the kids, like the mouthwatering pies delivered by the three cheeky sisters who owned one local restaurant. Blueberry, raspberry, cherry, blackberry, cranberry—the pies glistened and oozed in a delectable row on the kitchen counter, where Madam spotted them. "Oh, how nice!" she exclaimed in delight. She immediately sent a handwritten thank-you note, and the sisters soon showed up again, this time with all the ingredients to teach the children how to make crepes filled with raspberry jam. Madam came into the kitchen afterward to snag a couple. "It's so nice of them to do this for us," she remarked. Another gift of pies followed not long after that.

Then Nancy Tuckerman got a steep bill in the mail.

"Why are we ordering all these pies?" she demanded. The

shakedown wasn't just for the magically reappearing pies, either: It turns out that private crepe lessons cost a pretty penny, too. That was the last we saw of the sisters and their treats.

In town, people generally didn't make a big deal out of spotting us when we were browsing around in the souvenir shops or heading to the Melody Tent for the children's matinee on Saturdays, where live performances of shows like *Peter Pan* or *Alice in Wonderland* drew a crowd. The Secret Service, dressed in casual summer khakis instead of their usual dark suits, would sit in the row behind John and Caroline. They didn't make a big scene of it when some excited parent urged other children forward to "go say hello to John-John and Caroline." (John hated the nickname and no one in his family called him that—it came about when a White House reporter had once overheard the president call out to his toddler son twice in quick succession.) Caroline was bashful but still perfectly mirrored her mum's poise, replying with a simple yes and polite hello when anyone came up and asked, "Are you really Caroline Kennedy?" John saw everyone as a likely friend, though, and would go right up to strangers and introduce himself if I didn't stop him.

The children had been taught by their mother how to keep their heads down and their faces turned when paparazzi appeared and called out their names to try to get them to look at the cameras. I followed their example, and would also try my best to walk in front of the photographers to block their view, but they knew how to change position fast.

Unwelcome as that attention was, Madam never wanted John and Caroline treated like rare orchids in a greenhouse. They invited playmates over, and Caroline loved having slumber parties with her friends and cousins. Sandy used to bring some townie kids in to join the baseball games, and it wasn't unusual for the teenaged Kennedys to bring in friends who let younger siblings tag along to the compound for a day of fun. Sometimes Caroline and her favorite cousins, Courtney and Sydney, might set up a little lemonade stand on the road just outside the gates to sell nickel cups to the neighbor kids and their nannies. Not all encounters passersby had with Kennedy kids were so sweet and innocent, though.

The RFK crew were the real ringleaders when it came to mischief, with the four oldest—Kathleen, Joe, Bobby, and David—serving as the musketeers the rest were all too happy to follow. The bigger ones loved to hide up in the trees with water balloons to throw at cars or people going by on the narrow lanes skirting the compound. Kathleen, the eldest, was six years older than Caroline, and with younger siblings who just kept coming (eventually there were ten) she showed all the makings of a terrific general someday. Kathleen was very, very organized. She was the brains behind the water balloon munitions factory, directing the younger ones on the ground to help fill balloons, then ferry them by the bucketful to the older ones up in the branches. One day I caught a bunch of them sneaking up to the widow's walk at our house with dripping balloon bombs in hand. Our roof was the perfect foxhole for launching surprise balloon attacks on the Secret Service, the doddering gardener, or any other unsuspecting help passing below.

"I know you're having fun, but I don't want you up there," I told the kids.

"We're sorry," Caroline said with wide-eyed sincerity. Getting cross with her was impossible, and she knew it would take a lot more than a water balloon for me to tell her mother about any shenanigans.

"Well, don't do it again," I warned.

"We won't," she promised.

We both knew full well they'd just wait until I took my daily walk down to the beach at four o'clock, then sneak back upstairs again. Sure enough, when I went into Caroline's room to put away laundry sometime after lunch, I noticed the door to the widow's walk was ajar. Assuming another water balloon offensive was afoot, I latched the door closed again, figuring it would signal that I was on to them and send the mischievous little army into retreat while I took my customary stroll on the shore with Shannon.

As I walked back up to the house after my beach walk, I heard a voice calling to me from above.

"Kath! Kath! Could you please let me down?"

I looked up and saw Madam, waving to me from the widow's walk, a towel clutched to her chest. She had been up there sunbathing in her birthday suit when I locked the door! I hurried upstairs to free her, not volunteering that it was me who latched the door on her. She just laughed off her misadventure but had a handyman fix the door's lock so no one could get trapped up there again.

If she wasn't out swimming in the sea or jogging along the water's edge, Madam's favorite way to enjoy some alone time at the Cape was to paint at her easel in the sunroom, her feet bare, hair tied back with an elastic band, no makeup on her face. When it was just her in the evening, she liked to have her dinner in there on a tray. Her social life at the Cape was much less demanding than it was in Manhattan, with all its galas and charities and cultural events. When Madam entertained at the Cape, it was generally just other family members over for dinner—Jean and Stephen Smith, or Joan and Ted Kennedy, or Ethel. (Bobby was usually in Washington during the workweek and came up in time for the Saturday-morning touch-football games on the big lawn.)

Randolph Churchill, the son of the British prime minister, came for the weekend and ate with a cigarette still hanging from his mouth; he chain-smoked so furiously, even the sea breeze through the open windows couldn't cut through the haze. He coughed something terrible. Sometimes the men who had made up President Kennedy's inner White House circle, like former defense secretary Robert McNamara, Chuck Spalding, and Arthur Schlesinger, would come for a low-key reunion weekend together with Madam. They would all talk and laugh and smoke late into the night until the old friends drove back to their hotel rooms in town.

She seemed happy those nights, revisiting Camelot for a few lovely hours.

Madam also took special delight in visiting back and forth with her dear friend Bunny Mellon, who owned a spectacular mansion a short drive away. The Mellons were the richest of the rich, famous for their art collections and the Thoroughbred racehorses they bred in Virginia. Horses, fine art, and design were passions Madam shared with her friends, and Mrs. Mellon was the one Madam had turned to for help in restoring the White House. She was pressed into duty as a landscape designer, too, when President Kennedy had her reconfigure the famous Rose Garden. When Madam moved to New York after the assassination, Mrs. Mellon added her touch to Madam's apartment at 1040: "Charley, go easy on those rugs, they're Bunny Mellon's," I once overheard Madam tell the cleaning man as he ran the vacuum across the beautiful silk antique carpets in the dining room.

Mrs. Mellon was very ladylike and soft-spoken. She was quite tall and slim, and wore her hair in a fashionable but understated pageboy. When Mrs. Mellon was coming for lunch, Madam would go into a near-tizzy: Everything needed to be just right, even in the laid-back atmosphere at the Cape. "Kath, make sure the cushions are right on the chaise, that the zippers are to the back!" she'd fuss. In the kitchen, she would hover over the cook: What kind of soup was being served? Something with some green in it, she fretted, maybe some parsley or leek, or what about asparagus, was there any good asparagus?

You'd never guess Bunny Mellon was a billionaire the way she breezed through the kitchen door, chattering away, her arms full of flowers. Yellow sunflowers were her favorite offering.

"Kathy, come here, I want to show you how to cut these," she told me the first time she appeared with a bouquet at the Cape. "I need a sharp knife." I watched as she cut off the bottoms of each stem on the slant. "You don't go straight across," she explained. "They'll last much longer this way. Now you have to put an aspirin into the vase with the water."

I enjoyed arranging flowers and had a knack for doing the kind of loose, natural bouquets Madam fancied, but the surgery and aftercare Mrs. Mellon prescribed for the sunflowers were too much trouble for such big and raggedy-looking flowers, I thought.

On top of that, I'd have to listen to the cook go on and on about "ruining" a kitchen knife on the fat, fibrous stems. The blame would fall squarely on me, never Mrs. Mellon, who easily won over even the grouchiest of cooks with her sweet manner, always coming back to the kitchen the way she did to sing the praises of whatever soup she'd enjoyed for lunch. I liked Mrs. Mellon a great deal, but holy cow did I hate those sunflowers!

Flowers grew outside all the houses in the compound, of course, but the gardens varied in size and glory. Grandma Rose's was the most abundant, which was no surprise, since it took more plants to landscape around the big house. Ethel boasted the splashiest colors with her orange and magenta lilies, whose middles left yellow pollen all over the countertops. Madam had the most beautiful garden, though, since she had gone to the trouble of putting in a separate patch away from the house strictly for flowers. Mrs. Mellon had provided the cottage-style design, laying out what to plant and where. I would go out every morning to snip some lilies of the valley to place on Madam's breakfast tray. She loved their sweet, delicate fragrance.

Even though Madam grew plenty of her own fresh flowers, Grandma Rose would still summon me to her garden outside the big house.

"Send Jackie's girl over, I want her to cut some flowers for Jackie," she would tell whoever answered the pantry phone. Off I'd trot, shears in hand, and there would be Grandma Rose, waiting with hands on her hips in her flower garden to instruct me, stem by stem, which ones to cut. She wanted to make sure her daughter-in-law got only the nicest blooms. I don't know if she ever discovered that someone else was after the same thing.

Late at night, I knew, one of Jean Kennedy Smith's waitresses would sneak into Grandma's garden with a flashlight and scissors to snip some choice flowers for Mrs. Smith's house. She was very good at it and might have made a top-notch cat burglar if she'd taken her career in another direction. Since she was a friend of mine, I kept her secret, even after the Secret Service told me they'd spotted her swiping Madam's flowers as well. I didn't think it was anything worth creating a fuss over. Besides, I was hoping she would take the sunflowers I suspected Mrs. Mellon had planted in a back row: I had noticed the stalks growing ever taller and was dreading the attention they'd require once they bloomed. With no flowers to show, they looked like weeds poking up around the prettier plants surrounding them.

"Wilmer, when are those things going to bud?" I asked the ancient, half-blind gardener, who had no idea and couldn't have cared less. Wilmer spent much of his day picking up piles of dog poop and grumbling about all the Kennedy pets that ran free across the property.

One afternoon I happened to glance out the kitchen window and noticed a few teenaged cousins outside lurking by Madam's flower patch. The Secret Service guys sometimes came out of the trailer to toss a football or baseball around with them, so I thought nothing of it. Day after day, though, the kids kept coming back to the same spot, and they seemed to be pointing and looking at something in Madam's garden. Something was up, but I wasn't sure what. I went to investigate after the kids wandered off one afternoon but didn't see any evidence that they'd been back there sneaking beers or cigarettes or anything like that. The flowers hadn't been trampled, and the blasted, unblooming sunflowers were as big and healthy as ever, though there were little white buds on them now.

That's when it hit me. I went to find Jack Dempsey, the retired Cape police chief who often hung out at the Secret Service trailer.

"Jack, could you come take a look at something?" I asked. He followed me to the flower patch and, before I could even ask, confirmed my suspicions about the mystery stalks with a single glance.

"It's marijuana," he said. "How did it get here, do you know?"

"Well, I don't think the gardeners planted it," I replied.

"I have to tell Mrs. Kennedy," Dempsey said. He headed around the back of the house, toward the kitchen door. I knew Madam was out front on her porch, though, and hurried that way to head the police chief off at the pass. Better to prepare her for the news to come than give Dempsey the satisfaction of her initial reaction, whatever it was going to be.

"Madam, we just found marijuana growing in the flower patch," I breathlessly reported.

"Are you kidding me?" she said, her face registering disbelief. "Oh my God, this can't get out. What should we do?"

"Well, Jack Dempsey is in the kitchen and wants to talk to you," I told her.

She went to find him, and he took her outside to see for herself.

"What should we do about this?" she wondered again.

"Just ignore it, we'll pull it," Dempsey said. He and the Secret Service men ripped them up that afternoon. When I told Madam it had been taken care of, she nodded her approval. "Good," she said, reiterating her biggest concern: "I don't want this to get out." John and Caroline were much too young to have had any role in it, and while we all had a pretty good idea which cousins did, there was no confrontation, and no one got in any trouble.

Madam's house was by far the quietest in the compound, the one the other Kennedy mothers were most likely to seek out for a little break from the usual summer chaos. Joan liked to come play the grand piano, even though it was perpetually out of tune. Grandma would drop by before dinner, rosary in hand, to ask if Jackie would take a walk with her. "Oh no. Don't tell me she's here," Madam might say, sighing in resignation when I interrupted her painting or letter writing to say Rose was waiting, but she would dutifully get her own beads, and the two women would walk the perimeter of the compound until all sixty-plus prayers had been said. Rose went to Mass every morning, too, and would sometimes call to say she wanted Madam and the children to join her.

Grandma was constantly calling with messages to relay to Madam—*tell Jackie so-and-so is on television tonight and she should watch*—or detailed instructions about something she wanted done for her, and once she'd told you something, she'd want you to repeat it back to her. When I was over at the big house and Grandma got going, I'd start backing away down the path toward home until I got far enough that she couldn't shout loud enough for me to hear. She was strict and wanted things done exactly her way. She could ask five times what time the movie was starting in her basement theater that week, even though she was the one who mandated it begin at eight o'clock every single Friday. It wasn't senility—she was sharper than most of us, like a *Jeopardy!* champion the way she was always preparing history, geography, and current-event questions for everyone to answer at family dinners, or taking news clippings to discuss with her grandkids when they went for walks together. The hectoring about what we would be doing and at precisely what time had more to do with Rose always needing to somehow pin down the future. What she couldn't control had cost her so much already.

The Friday-night movies in Rose's basement were a highlight of the week for everyone, staff included. The theater was down a long hallway filled with Rose's collection of dolls from around the world, all in glass display cases. I never saw any of the grand-daughters playing with any of them, and the untouchable collection reminded me of the Christmas doll that Briege and I had once gotten from America.

Wilmer was in charge of running the movie projector, but the gardener's glasses always slipped off and the film would get jammed up. All the help were invited, but the unwritten rule was to wait until the Kennedys had taken their prime seats in the back rows first. Our seats were down in the front, close to the screen. The film started promptly at eight o'clock—Grandma's rule—and if you came in a minute late, you had to crawl on the floor to get to your seat so you didn't block anyone's view. The movies would always start and stop, start and stop, with long pauses while Wilmer tried to figure out how to rethread the film. Usually one of Bobby and Ethel's boys got up to go help him and get it running again. The wait was well worth the chance to see big box-office hits that were playing in the theaters at the same time, like *Georgy Girl* and *Midnight Cowboy*.

The real fun for the staff came on Thursdays, though, when most everyone had the day off. All the waitresses, cooks, govern-esses, and the girls Ethel would import from Ireland as summer help ("the Irish bunnies," Senator Kennedy would call them) would gather at the beach to clamber aboard Joseph P. Kennedy's yacht, the *Marlin*, which became our party boat for the day. A local charter captain and his handsome teenaged son, Dicky, would take us to nearby Nantucket, Martha's Vineyard, or Provincetown. We'd leave at ten in the morning, lugging coolers full of sandwiches and whatever leftovers the kitchen staffs had scored. Some of the older help would also bring thermoses of cocktails they'd made themselves by raiding the liquor cabinets of their respective employers. I was a teetotaler myself back then. I didn't even like the smell of beer or alcohol, and I wasn't of legal age anyway. We had a portable radio to play Top Forty hits off the AM radio stations when we got reception, and we'd sunbathe on deck to the Righteous Brothers and Herman's Hermits and Sam the Sham and the Pharaohs. We'd spend the afternoon wandering around one of the quaint, pretty tourist towns, eating ice-cream cones and shopping for souvenirs. Everything was pricey at the height of the season, but we could always find some little thing to spend a few dollars on, like the nautical rope bracelets that were so popular. We'd soak and soften them in water, then bleach them with Clorox so they'd fade and look worn. John and Caroline used to wear them all the time, too. They never did seem to go out of style. We'd head back as the sun washed the horizon in watercolor shades of pink and violet, docking in time to spend a glorious summer evening on the boardwalk, eating burgers and fries or fresh boiled shrimp and corn on the cob. When we really wanted to make a night of it, we would head to one of the local clubs to go dancing.

I was still underage my first summer at the Cape—I wouldn't turn twenty-one until December—but one night when we were all going out to listen to music, one of the Irish bunnies had her sister's ID that she offered to let me use to get inside the club. We figured the Irish all looked alike, or close enough, anyway, in American eyes. We wriggled into our cutest miniskirts and swiped on pale frosted lipstick that made us look like we'd been frozen. Provi always took the longest to get ready, wanting her hair to be perfect and her pretty face flawless. She was always borrowing my Cover Girl foundation—trying, I figured, to hide the twenty extra years she had on most of us. As we stood in line outside the club that night, I grew more and more nervous the closer we got to the bouncer. I could see him carding people. When it was my turn, he studied the Irish bunny's sister's ID for a moment, then shook his head.

"She can't come in," he said in a voice too low for the others to hear, gesturing behind me with a tilt of his chin.

I didn't understand what he meant. I glanced over my shoulder, trying to see whatever it was he had seen that had led to this decision, but all I saw was Provi, waiting impatiently with the others.

"Sorry, the ID didn't work," I lied to everyone. "They won't let me in." We all left.

I never told Provi she was the one being turned away, that my foundation hadn't lightened her skin enough to fool the bouncer charged with making sure only white people were let in to dance.

I came to the United States the year the Civil Rights Act was signed into law, but *segregation* wasn't a word I even knew. I had no clue at all what it was about. I brought the newspapers to Madam each morning but never read them myself. I always hated reading in school and wasn't much good at it. Whatever I learned, I picked up listening to the conversations of the more educated people around me.

I spent my summers in the privileged world of yacht clubs and private beaches, never knowing that race riots were erupting in major cities across the country at the same time, worse with each passing year. I wasn't in college, signing petitions, or rallying for a protest march, nor was I spending my day in an office build-ing then going to happy hour with my coworkers come five o'clock to talk about what was going on in America. My days re-volved around Madam's wants and needs, never mine. I didn't have a life that was wholly my own.

I lived instead inside Camelot's last bubble, too blind to see that this was a far different Kennedy era.

It was Bobby's time now.

SIX

Queen of the Land

Settling back into the rhythms and routines of 1040 took some effort after the summer-camp atmosphere of the Cape, and doubling as governess on top of serving as Madam's personal assistant became more demanding once school and all of the kids' activities in the city got under way. Madam kept offering me the permanent job as Maud's successor, and I kept turning it down. If you were assigned to the kids full-time, you couldn't leave in the evening if Madam was going out, and your schedule was too unpredictable to make plans of your own. Sticking with my original job gave me a better chance of at least occasionally getting the evenings or monthly weekends off that I had been promised when I was hired.

The problem was, there was no such thing as a time clock to punch. I was on duty until Madam decided I wasn't.

"Kath, could you come here for a minute?"

The request always came after dinner, just when I thought my long day was done and it might be safe to slip out the door to enjoy the rest of my evening, maybe see if Bridey Sullivan or my sister Briege were free, too. Instead, I would end up shrugging off my coat to go find Madam in whichever room she was no doubt about to redecorate. Hanging and rehanging pictures was her favorite thing to do when the house was quiet and still. Her art collection was huge and ever changing, and she loved to rearrange it. If it wasn't the paintings, it was clothes she wanted to move around from one closet to another, or shoes that needed reorganizing in the middle of the night. She was often restless in those hours between the children's bedtime and her own, and it wasn't until I became a wife myself that I understood how lonely nine o'clock can be. There's a world of difference between talking about life over a glass of wine with your spouse and thinking about life over a glass alone.

It couldn't have been so urgent at that hour for Madam to have me hold some heavy painting of a huntsman on horseback and move it higher, no, lower, while she made a pencil mark on the wall and hammered in a nail, but I felt I had no choice but to indulge her. I had even missed out on celebrating my twenty-first birthday with friends when she decided with no advance notice that she was going to her country home in Peapack to spend a few days horseback riding and that I had to come along to watch the children. Once we were there, she caught wind of my birthday from one of the other girls on staff I'd been planning to celebrate with. I was touched when Madam went out of her way to make me feel special, surprising me with a strawberry and whipped cream cake and some lovely gifts—two turtleneck sweaters, a suede purse from Caroline, and a silver cigarette holder from John—but I also resented living my life almost entirely on her terms. I was a full-fledged adult now, and it was only natural to want to start spreading my wings.

What I really needed to do was to take a page from Mugsy's book and learn how to stand up for myself when Madam took advantage. The first time I saw Mugsy push back was one afternoon when the crusty old Secret Service man had returned weighed down like a pack mule with fancy shopping bags after Madam went on a spree. She hadn't been home but a few minutes before she asked me to summon Mugsy back upstairs. She had one of her heavy horse pictures in hand, and I knew what was coming next. Mugsy reappeared with blood in his eye.

"How did you like your lunch today, Madam?" he asked evenly.

"I didn't have lunch," she breezily replied.

"And neither did I! We were out all day and you didn't give me a break to get something to eat," Mugsy complained. "I'm going to get my lunch first, and you'll have to wait about your picture!"

"You probably had your lunch, Mugsy, but go ahead. Go and have your lunch!" she snapped back, the sarcasm turning her breathy voice into pure acid. Mugsy stormed out of the room. I stood there shocked. *That's the last we'll be seeing of him*, I thought, certain that Mrs. Tuckerman would be waiting down in the lobby with his walking papers the second Mugsy stepped out of the elevator. Instead, he was back the next day.

"Good morning, Mugsy!" Madam greeted him sweetly. Mugsy was all smiles, too. Everything was forgotten, and they just carried on until their next fight, when the pattern would repeat itself. They both seemed to enjoy the bickering.

The closest I'd ever come to defiance was unintentional, and had more to do with manners than moxie. I'd put my hair up in pink rollers and tied a scarf over them while doing some chores back in the servants' wing one morning, thinking it didn't matter, since no one but the staff or kids would see me. But Madam did, and I was swiftly brought to heel:

"Kath, I don't need to be seeing you in those rollers ever again," she reprimanded me. I apologized and went to take them out. I had rolled her thick, jet hair in curlers many a time and set her up with magazines and refreshments while she baked under her hooded dryer in the guest room when she was between appointments with her celebrity hairdresser, Mr. Kenneth. (If her roots were showing, she touched them up herself with a bottle of tint Mr. Kenneth mixed up for her to keep at home.)

It stung to be put back in my place, but I accepted she had every right to do so. I just couldn't muster the nerve or heart to do the same when the tables were turned and she was reeling me back in after I'd already said good night and changed out of my uniform. Exasperated as I was by her last-minute tasks and the way it was never "just for a minute," I sensed it wasn't my talent for hammering in a picture hook she wanted in those empty hours so much as my simple presence. I was helping keep vigil. Over what was never talked about.

What I preferred to be doing when the day was done was exactly what every other single young New Yorker was doing: going out to unwind with friends. I was madly in love with the city, and it hadn't taken long for me and Briege to discover its lively immigrant scene. All the doormen and domestics and other young working-class Irish came out to play in social clubs that sprang up like Brigadoon for a few merry hours every night in space rented from some dive bar or union hall. Our favorite was the Jaeger Haus, which was as Irish as a Wiener schnitzel, but the Germans retreated when it was our turn to cut loose, and it felt like I was back at the Friday-night dances in Inniskeen, doing the twist until my knees ached. Call it the twist, the chicken, the swim, or whatever you like, it was all basically one big Irish mating dance. The courting ritual was much more brutal and the competition more fierce than it had been on Inniskeen's dance floor, though, especially when the handsome, smooth-talking Italians would show up. The Irish girls lapped up their Casanova charm and swagger. The Irish lads didn't appreciate the competition, though, and after exchanging some choice insults about national soccer leagues, fists would fly while Motown played in the background. The Irish always won. And the Italians always came back another night.

The cloakroom at the Jaeger Haus was where you really figured out the lay of the land. You had to squeeze past all the coats to get to the ladies' room, and there was no slipping by Maryann, the nosy coat check girl, without getting interrogated.

"Oh, Kathleen, what happened?" she'd ask with syrupy fake concern. "No one asked you to dance?"

Maryann knew the bathroom was where the wallflowers and rejects hid, applying lipstick until another song started up so they could go back out without the humiliation of being on public display while standing around waiting to be picked. The loo was also where romances were analyzed like soap operas, dramatic mid-waltz breakups were plotted, and other interesting secrets occasionally spilled. The only girls who never hid out in the bathroom were the ones who looked like Jean Shrimpton or danced like

Ginger Rogers. I didn't check either of those boxes. I was terrific with hair and makeup, though, and once I got the hang of copying Madam's style on a budget (long ribbed turtlenecks belted over a hip-hugger miniskirt with boots was the easiest to pull off), I may not have made the Most Beautiful list, but I could always pull off cute.

There was no denying I was a terrible dancer, though. At five foot seven, I always ended up having to be the man when practicing with my shorter sister or friends. Problem was, I had gotten too good at it. "I'm the leader, you're not!" I was constantly being scolded by the frustrated guys who asked me to dance. I wasn't schooled in the art of playing the helpless female, either: The first time a gentleman tried to hold my coat for me back in the cloakroom, I grabbed it back, startled by some stranger touching me, my adrenaline surging at the muscle memory of old Putty groping me when I was twelve.

"Give me my coat!" I cried in alarm.

"I'm only helping you so you can get your arm in the sleeve!" the poor guy protested.

Needless to say, I spent my fair share of time in that ladies' room pretending my lipstick needed fixing.

Thanks to an intervention by Madam, though, my self-confidence was starting to build.

After a brisk, steady parade of ill-tempered and uninspired cooks, Madam had finally landed a gem: Annemarie was a vivacious young German who was just a year older than I was. We hit it off right away. I could tell Madam liked her, too, sometimes even sitting to have a cup of coffee and chat while we were all in the kitchen. As much as I liked Annemarie, though, I also felt a pang of envy: She always looked so fresh and pretty, with the kind of figure that could carry off the bold colors, short hemlines, and geometric prints that were all the rage. She showed me the Upper East Side thrift shop she had discovered where all the rich women donated their clothes. Annemarie even knew how to dress in satin and fur for a pittance. Fashion was fun and daring in the mid-1960s, but I felt too frumpy and depressed to join the revolution. I had ballooned to 185 pounds in America, and I wasn't even twenty-three years old. It had been easy to forget how big I'd gotten when the other females on Madam's staff were twice my age and just as heavy, but Annemarie was a daily reminder of how I should be, and what I longed to be.

I was disgusted with myself, and my spiraling self-esteem put me in a funk that Madam quickly noticed.

"Kath, is something wrong?" she asked me one morning as I was laying out whatever stylish outfit she had requested from her closet that day. Without warning, I found myself fighting tears, and I blurted out the truth.

"I hate the way I look! I wish I could have a figure like yours,

Madam," I said. "You always look so beautiful, whatever you put on! I wish I could lose some weight."

"Oh, Kath," Madam sympathized, "I can help you with that, if you want. Come with me." Hopeful and curious, I followed her as she led me into the kitchen.

"Annemarie," she said, "Kathy wants to lose some weight, and you and I are going to help her. Can you fix some special meals for her?"

Annemarie readily agreed, and the two of them quickly mapped out a new eating regimen for me: a boiled egg and tea in the morning, cottage cheese with an apple or other fresh fruit at lunch, and a poached chicken breast or piece of fish with a salad or steamed vegetables for dinner. Plain yogurt when I wanted a snack. Annemarie also kept a large jug filled with water in the fridge, and insisted I drink eight large glasses a day. The diet was almost exactly what Madam herself ate at home when she wasn't entertaining.

No wonder she stayed so slim despite the rich food served at the fancy restaurants and lavish parties scattered across her social calendar!

The diet began that day at lunchtime, and with Annemarie's encouragement, I stuck to it (minus a few Yodels pilfered from the box in the pantry meant for John and Caroline). I even figured out how to make the plain yogurt not taste like wet chalk by mixing in a spoonful of instant coffee powder.

The pounds steadily melted away, and after six months, I was forty pounds lighter and actually eager to try on clothes and show off my reclaimed figure!

Browsing happily through the racks of discounted designer clothes at Loehmann's, I found myself a form-fitting maroon knit dress, which even garnered praise from Madam about how smart I looked. I never wanted to let go of that dress after that—I wore it until it was threadbare and long out of style. My work uniforms were another story, though: A few sizes too big now, they hung on me like potato sacks, and I asked if it might be all right to order new ones in lavender—my favorite color—instead of white.

"Of course!" Madam said, promptly buying me two—one lavender and another in a pale blush rose. She of all people understood what self-esteem could do for a woman. Keeping herself fit, active, and impeccably groomed had to have helped carry her through the challenges life threw her way, it stood to reason. Without really realizing it, I began to take on those habits myself, much the way a younger sister mirrors the older one she envies and admires.

At the Irish clubs, my newfound confidence and more stylish wardrobe didn't go unnoticed among the girls gossiping in the ladies' room.

"Who do you think you are now, Jacqueline Kennedy?" one of them ribbed me good-naturedly.

"Not really, but I'm trying," I answered honestly. Besides taking some cues from Madam's closet, I had also adopted some of her mannerisms, like the way she would absently hold her sunglasses in one hand and twirl them by the stem, or wear them on top of her head to push the hair back from her face. Actually, it was more than the gesture I'd borrowed—I'd also picked up a couple pairs of the big, round sunglasses themselves when she threw them out.

The girls at the Irish club weren't the only ones to notice the new me: I landed myself a boyfriend, too. Pat had a good job delivering oil, and he was a real gentleman, taking me out and treating me to dinners and movies. He was easygoing and fit in well with my sister and friends. Everyone thought he was good marriage material. There was just one drawback, and it was a big one: Pat told me that he could never live in Ireland again. His allergies just couldn't take the damp. I felt bad for him, but this news was too big a disappointment for me to brush aside. My interest in him swiftly began to fizzle. The whole reason I didn't date American men, or any of the flirty Italians, was because I had every intention of returning home someday to raise a family of my own. An Irish husband seemed like the best way to guarantee that future. If I fell for an American who didn't want to uproot himself, I would never get back.

Much as I loved America, I considered it a holding pattern until my "real" life took flight. I was proud to be able to send money home each month, as well as care packages of new Levi's for my brothers and a nice dress for Mam, but my younger siblings were old enough to hold down jobs of their own now, too, and the situation wasn't as bleak as it had been when Briege and I were sent abroad. I didn't have to stay forever. Returning on my own as a single girl was out of the question, however. The ones who did that got branded as failures.

Despite our geographical divide, Pat and I continued to coast along, and my resolve faltered. There was no romantic proposal or anything, but at some point, it was just understood that we were headed toward marriage. Then our general discussions turned into a specific decision, and we set a date a few months down the road. I even reserved the church.

The plans came to a screaming halt when Pat announced that he didn't believe in engagement rings. He considered them a waste of money.

"Do you think it's wrong that it matters so much to me?" I asked Bridey. The ring was supposed to be a symbol, and a sparkling diamond—even a small one—showed the world that I was treasured. Pat wasn't at all a cheapskate, which somehow made his position about the ring all the more hurtful: I felt like he had done his calculating and concluded I wasn't worth that level of investment. Yet here I was, giving up Ireland for him! Bridey understood what I meant, but her reservations about me marrying Pat had nothing to do with my neglected ring finger. Why would I want to tie myself down at twenty-two? she wanted to know. The more I thought about it, the more I saw how right Bridey was. I called Pat up and told him the wedding was off. He had known I was miffed about the ring but never expected it to blow up this way. Neither had I, frankly. The decision felt right, but I was deeply embarrassed by how I had let my indignation take control of delivering the news to Pat, who called me back later, baffled and angry.

I agreed to meet him for coffee to explain.

"I'm sorry," I said, and meant it. Hurting him felt awful. "I changed my mind. I'm too young. I have more single life to live."

Pat was still furious, but there was nothing to be done. I had expected to feel devastated—a broken engagement should have warranted at least a brief Wonder Bread relapse—but the crying jags, mayo sandwiches, and country music sing-alongs with my pillow never came. Maybe I hadn't been in love after all. It was scary to think how close I'd just come to making a lifelong commitment to someone out of mere fondness and the fear, maybe, that I would end up alone. I had hung enough pictures in the middle of the night to know that all the riches in the world couldn't ease that ache.

It was back to the dance floor for me.

Wedding or no, I still yearned to nest. I was desperate to set down stakes on that "real" life I imagined building for myself. Bridey was itchy to escape Kennedy-land once in a while, too, devoted as she was to Jean Kennedy Smith's two little boys, William and Stephen. We decided to look for an apartment to share. We soon found a one-bedroom flat on East Eighty-first Street just a couple of blocks from the river, making the mayor one of our new neighbors. The beautiful park surrounding Gracie Mansion became a favorite spot for me to get some sun and daydream when I had a free afternoon.

Our apartment was a tiny fifth-floor walkup with a water closet. There was no shower, just a bathtub in the kitchen, but we didn't mind brushing our teeth in the kitchen sink. We didn't plan to live there full-time, anyway. All we wanted was a cozy place to relax and have friends over when we could. I would still sleep at 1040 during my workweek for convenience's sake, and Bridey, as governess, had to spend the night at Mrs. Smith's as long as she was on duty. We split our $75 monthly rent down the middle, and when Briege began hanging out so much that we threatened to charge her, she ponied up for the utilities instead.

Briege also came in handy with the used sewing machine she had bought, whipping out kitchen curtains and a tablecloth from cheap fabric we got at Woolworth's. I dug into my savings to buy a double bed for the bedroom, and Bridey provided a couch for the living area. We slapped a piece of plywood over the bathtub and it became our table. Friends would come over to play Parcheesi or 25, Ireland's national card game. Like bridge, 25 involves lots of rules and lots of math. We would toast pieces of pita bread and butter them to snack on over endless mugs of tea.

I didn't breathe a word to Madam about getting my own place, and Bridey kept the apartment a secret from Mrs. Smith, too. The whole point of having it was so they couldn't find us.

Fall and winter with Madam were always filled with lots of little trips. We might have Thanksgiving with Madam's mother at the Auchincloss estate in Newport, Rhode Island, where I tasted my first roasted chestnut and thought I'd died and gone to heaven, or head off to Colorado for a family-reunion ski vacation while the kids were on Christmas break. Madam took me to Bloomingdale's and bought me a thick Irish sweater, a puffy black parka, plus matching pants, gloves, scarf, and boots.

Aspen was like no place I could ever have even imagined, as close to an exact opposite of Ireland as could be with its fields of deep white snow, towering Rocky Mountains, and jet-set image. Setting out with our Secret Service detail that first morning in my new winter outfit, I quickly discovered that I was no ski bunny. I was too scared to even get on the ski lift, much less come rocketing back down an icy mountain on two skinny pieces of wood.

Fortunately, John was still a beginner at the time, so I was able to hang out on the sidelines watching him take lessons on lower ground. The poor Secret Service man guarding him had nothing but a government-issued jacket and no gloves. Since my puffy parka had nice, warm pockets, I loaned the agent my new leather gloves so his trigger finger wouldn't get frostbite in the event he needed it. (I never did get those gloves back; I guess that was my contribution to national security.)

I was much happier back at our chalet, sipping hot cocoa with marshmallows with the kids or sitting around the big table with everyone for one of the family's trivia contests. There'd be twenty or more of them. They were all very big on games, and they wouldn't allow you to sit out. Any sore losers or crybabies were told to go to their rooms. The trivia contests petrified me: I had no idea which states started with the letter C or the names of the world's biggest mountain or longest bridge. You'd get a poker chip for every answer you got right. Caroline and Courtney always had the biggest stacks, though Bobby was the undisputed king. I'd sit next to Courtney and elbow her as my turn approached. "You'll be fine, Kat!" she promised, always slipping me the right answer in the nick of time. She and Caroline even knew the answers to more of the questions about Ireland than I did.

When the parents went out for the evening, the nightly all-cousin pillow fight began. It was like indoor touch football with the same amount of running, tackling, shouting, and laughing, plus feathers. So many feathers, it looked like we were inside one of those little souvenir snow globes and someone had given us a ferocious shake. I tried to pull John out of the fray—feathers triggered his asthma, and I was worried he'd have a coughing fit—but he seemed fine, so I let him have his fun.

Beautiful as Aspen was, when it came to family trips, New Jersey was much more my speed. Madam leased a house in Peapack, the heart of hunt country. She loved to spend weekends riding to the hounds with her fellow equestrians or just cantering through the leafy back roads. She boarded her horse at the stables of her good friends Peggy and Murray McDonnell. The McDonnells had a houseful of children for John and Caroline to play with, too.

Peapack was about fifty miles from Manhattan, but it felt five times as far when Mugsy was driving. Going to the Cape was even worse. The other Secret Service guys had warned me to use the restroom first because Mugsy never stopped until he was out of gas, but poor Shannon couldn't hold it that long, and I'd always end up begging Mugsy to stop so the dog didn't pee in the backseat. The road trips were made even more insufferable by Mugsy's smelly cigars and his mistaken belief that we would prefer to hear him singing old Sinatra standards over listening to the radio. If he wasn't in the mood to torture Frank's greatest hits, Mugsy would opt for torturing John instead, with an old song called "Arrah Go On I'm Gonna Go Back to Oregon."

"Pat McCarty, hale and hearty, living in Oregon . . . ," he'd begin.

"Nooo, Mugsy! Stop!" John would plead from the backseat, knowing that Mugsy not only intended to recite the whole silly song about a cheap Irishman, but also wouldn't stop repeating it until John correctly recited it himself.

"Heard a lotta talk about the great New Yawk, so he sold his farm when all was calm, and landed on old Broadway."

"Nooo, pleeeeease!"

The ditty ended with Pat taking a girl into a "swell café"— Mugsy always drew out the *swelllll* to annoy John even more— and getting sticker shock.

"The waiter brought the card and said 'what will you have' to Pat; then Pat looked at the prices and he said 'I'll have me hat.'"

"C'mon, John, now you say it," Mugsy would urge. If John messed up a line, Mugsy would make him start all over again, or recite it again himself. Back and forth they'd go, until John clapped his hands over his ears. "Mugsy, if you say it again, I'm going to jump out of the car!" he warned. Caroline would ignore the whole thing, letting whatever book she was reading carry her away to some more interesting place.

The Peapack house was too small to bring a cook—I had to share a room with John as it was—so Madam and I did all the shopping and made the meals. In those close quarters without a houseful of staff, our relationship felt cozier and more familiar. She shed the trappings of her usual pampered life at 1040 with ease, preferring to keep it simple in Peapack. We cooked together—just us and the kids—sticking to things like spaghetti with Ragu from a can, or hot dogs or fish sticks. Madam had a habit of wandering off and forgetting she had something on the stove, though, so there was a good chance a pot would boil over or the noodles would be gummy if one of the kids or I didn't catch it in time. She could boil an egg all right, but it was probably going to end up hard-boiled. We were more inclined to laugh and eat our mistakes than start all over. Oddly enough, she could make a perfect pot of Irish tea— boiling water poured over double bags and steeped just right so it was nice and strong. (She taught me to save the used bags and cool them in the freezer so she could put them over her eyes after her morning shower, to get rid of puffiness.) I was no Julia Child myself, but I let her play head chef in Peapack. I was reluctant to show any skills in the kitchen at all beyond my radar vision for leftovers in the fridge.

"Never let them see you know how to cook, or that'll just be one more thing they'll be expecting you to do," my sister had wisely advised me when we both started working as live-ins. If you didn't set boundaries and guard them fiercely, you would just keep giving away more and more of yourself, 'til one day there wasn't a you left at all.

In the spring of 1967, Madam came to me with news of a big trip in the works.

"Kath, you're going to love where we're going," she teased, her eyes dancing.

"Where, Madam?" I hoped it was someplace tropical and warm. Hawaii was supposed to be beautiful. Coconuts dropping right off the trees.

"Ireland! We're going to bring you back where you came from!"

No coconuts and suntan lotion there, but she was right—I was excited. We'd be vacationing with the McDonnell family for six whole weeks. With regular days off and the alternate weekends I was supposed to have, I could squeeze in some good visits with my family. I couldn't wait to dash off a letter to Mam to let her know.

Very, very excited to be coming home, I wrote, *and guess who with?*

I'd had my first trip back to Inniskeen just the previous summer, but it had been bittersweet. Dad had died right as I started working for Madam. His heart had given out and he had been buried two weeks before Uncle Pat even broke the news to me. "There's nothing you could do anyway, and you were starting your new job," he rationalized. He was right. I wouldn't have been able to afford airfare back to Ireland, and taking leave right as I was being hired could have given Madam second thoughts about my reliability.

I wept alone in my room after hearing the news, never telling

Madam of my loss for fear it would just scrape at her own wound. She had a keen sense for sorrow, though, and she had picked up on mine right away, hovering about and asking if I was happy working for her, assuming that Provi's high-handedness was at the root of my melancholy. I was thrilled that another trip to Ireland was on the near horizon, and a grand tour, at that. This one would be a happier homecoming, to be sure. Ireland would do both our hearts good.

After stepping off onto the tarmac to cheering crowds at Shannon Airport, we all headed to the Waterford coast aboard a chartered luxury bus with big picture windows that the children excitedly waved from as we rolled through villages whose narrow lanes were lined with well-wishers. What was so familiar to me—cows crossing a cobbled road, spring lambs gamboling in velvet green fields—was new and thrilling to John and Caroline. The Kennedy clan had steeped the kids in their Irish heritage from the time they were babes, and they had grown up hearing the music, folktales, and brogues of the Irish help around them. Caroline wore a green ribbon in her hair every St. Patrick's Day. At seven, John probably had a better grasp of Irish geography than American, loving to moderate fake debates among Madam's staff about our heritage.

"Which is better, Monaghan or Sligo?" he would goad May and me as he sat at the kitchen table with his cookies and milk after school.

"Monaghan's farmland is more fertile," I began.

"Sligo was the home of William Butler Yeats!" May boasted.

"Point to Kathy!" John shouted. Potatoes trumped poets in this game, I was glad to learn.

"But Sligo is so much prettier," May objected. That was true enough, but I had my pride and wasn't about to agree.

"Go on, May, they're still working the fields with donkeys in Sligo," I scoffed. What I lacked in ammunition, I made up for with typically barbed Irish humor.

"Two points Kathy!" John shouted again, slapping his hand on the table this time for emphasis.

John's appreciation for Monaghan's agricultural talents had been reinforced by my great success in showing him how to grow an avocado tree by putting the pit in a glass of water and letting it sprout roots. John was excited when I told him it was time to plant it. We found an empty ceramic pot abandoned in the back hallway after its plant had died, and we commandeered it for our avocado.

"Between you and me, we'll take care of it," I told John. We checked it every day. First a shoot came up, then a leaf, than another. John loved watering it, and before long, we had a big, healthy tree. We kept it by the back elevator. One day, I spotted Charley hauling it through the front hallway.

"Where're you going with that?" I demanded.

"Madam said put it on the front patio out the living room," he answered.

"No, no, no, Charley! That's not her plant, that's my plant—it belongs to me and John," I explained. Charley put the avocado tree back.

Guests were coming for lunch that day, and Madam wanted to know why Charley hadn't moved the big plant yet. Charley wasted no time pointing the finger at me.

"I was bringing it and she said it was hers," he said.

"Why is *her* plant in *my* pot?" Madam countered. "Bring it out here."

"Madam," I jumped in, "that plant's been here a year!"

I lost the avocado tug-of-war, and without John and me babying it every day, the little tree died of neglect in its new location. Nonetheless, I was still eager for John and Caroline—born and raised city kids—to see what rural life was really like and share what I knew about planting and harvesting when we all visited my homeland.

On the way out the door for our Ireland trip, John had tossed poor old May a small bone: "Don't worry, May, I'll go see for myself if Monaghan is better and let you know."

Monaghan and Sligo were both north of the route we took across the country then down the western coast, passing through an Ireland I was seeing myself for the first time, before we finally pulled up to the secluded estate where we would be spending the summer. Irish step dancers in traditional costume were waiting to greet us alongside servants standing at attention in black-and-white uniforms outside a white Georgian mansion. Horses and ponies grazed in the front pasture. Inside, a parquet entry hall unfurled for what seemed like a city block. There were fifteen bedrooms in all, with Madam's in the front, facing the Irish Sea.

Point to Waterford, I thought.

Madam had a busy calendar with jaunts here and there, including a state dinner at Dublin Castle, where she wowed the fashion world yet again, her dark hair and eyes offering dramatic contrast to her vivid green evening gown. She stayed overnight at the presidential palace and went to the Irish Sweeps Derby the next day to watch the Thoroughbreds race. I stayed behind at Woodstown House with the children and the McDonnells, enjoying our lazy days picnicking in the fields or climbing down the rocky cliffs to play on the beach.

"Tell us again about the fairies and leprechauns," Caroline would beg me as the three of us ate our sandwiches on a blanket we'd spread over the soft grass. Inniskeen was a day's journey to the north, but watching John and Caroline enjoying exactly what I had loved to do at their age, in this same land, carried me on a sweet, nostalgic breeze back to my own childhood.

"If you sit on a hill at night and are very quiet, sometimes you can hear the crackling of sticks and see their little fires," I told the children. "I spotted them once or twice from a distance doing a jig and smoking their pipes. Sometimes they just sit round a circle playing cards or other games. But if you get too close, they vanish."

Tell us more, they would demand. *Can we catch one?* They had big plans to hunt for pots of gold on this trip and were desperate for any clue.

"You have to look for a lone blackthorn bush in the middle of a field," I instructed them. "That's where the fairy forts are. All the farmers know it's bad luck to cut the bush down. Sometimes when they're plowing their fields around it, they find little clay pipes, two or three inches long, with heads the size of a marble. You can cut a single branch from the lone bush for a shillelagh or walking stick, but that's all. The fairies live under the bush or beneath stones nearby."

I had spotted a lone blackthorn in a field from the bus window on the way to Woodstown, and pointed it out to John and Caroline. They spotted a few on their own over the course of our summer as we hiked the hills and fields of the Woodstown estate. Off they would run to search for cold fairy campfires or tiny decks of Old Maid. Leprechauns were trickier, I had informed them. They loved playing pranks and stealing potatoes or small tools from farmers' sheds, probably to dig holes for burying their black pots of gold coins.

"I'm going to catch one," John vowed.

"Nobody ever has," I replied.

He spent the day concocting various plans to outsmart the leprechauns. He vowed to sneak up on them with a net, or ambush them with an empty shoe box or such. No way would he be returning to America empty-handed!

I told the children less fanciful tales, too, sharing my favorite memories from a childhood that couldn't be more different from their own. I recounted how Easter Sunday had always been such a glorious holiday, because my brothers and sisters and I got to take the jar of pennies and half-pennies Aunt Bridge saved for us and go to the shops on the road to buy candy. We always gave up candy for Lent and looked forward to this binge when our sugar fast was over. We'd pour the coins out on the counter and buy as many little chocolate eggs and pink marshmallow ducks as we could. We'd gather a dozen eggs from Mam's hens and bring a saucepan from home, along with tea, matches, and a bit of milk. We'd make ourselves a little stove from sticks and stones, fill our pan with river water, and boil the eggs for lunch. We used the cleaner water from the spring for our milk-tea. Our friends would come along with their own Easter candy. One boy who was better off than the rest of us—Bryan was his name—always had good chocolate, and he would trade us some Cadbury for boiled eggs.

We were gone all day, and life seemed absolutely perfect.

Tell us about the animals, Kat!

Both John and Caroline were devoted animal lovers—besides trusty Shannon (a gift from Ireland, from President Kennedy's last trip) there was a menagerie of birds, guinea pigs, and snakes back at 1040, plus the horses and ponies at the country home in New Jersey. They were politely interested but not nearly as impressed by their private tours of castles and kissing the Blarney Stone as they were with the invitations by local farms to visit the sheep pen or a sty full of squealing piglets. They begged me to tell them stories about all the animals when I was growing up on a farm. Their favorite was the one my older siblings and I came to remember as the famous Billy Goat Incident. (If only we'd had the technology then that we do today to instantly record life's silliest moments, we no doubt would have become global Internet sensations.)

The goat was a mean and smelly one, even by goat standards, and we came across him standing in the road one day on the way to school with our third cousins, the Kirks. The goat bleated and charged us, and the game was on, all of us teasing him to see how riled up he would get, until a passerby came along and put a stop to it. He took the goat and tied him with a rope to an electric pole out in the field. We went on our merry way, but my brother Mick couldn't stop thinking about the poor goat tethered and alone out there, so that night, he snuck back to the field and cut the rope. The goat was loose again.

And waiting in the road for us the next morning.

This time, he chased us all the way to school, much to our delight. But as we ran inside the schoolhouse, the goat kept running, too, right into our classroom, where he proceeded to wreak havoc, upending desks and scattering books. The children were all laughing and hollering and shrieking, while Mr. Mullen, in a red-faced rage, chased the goat around the room. He finally ripped the chalkboard off the wall to fling at the wretched beast. The goat caught it with his horns, and Mr. Mullen took advantage of the momentary disarmament to shove him back outside. That wasn't really the end of him, though: Male goats have a bad-enough musky stink to them to begin with, but when a buck is in rut, he'll spray himself liberally with his own urine as a sort of goat aftershave to attract the females. This one had spared no expense in that department, and the room reeked with the awful stench for what seemed like weeks afterward. We never saw him again, though.

Once the goat had departed, Mr. Mullen went straight for his hated strap—a small whip with not just one thick strip of leather, but two. "Smiths and Kirks, line up and put out your hands," he ordered. The red welts he raised burned for days. Corporal punishment wasn't expressly allowed in public schools, mind you, but none of us ever told our parents about Mr. Mullen's cruelty because we would've just gotten punished a second time at home for incurring the teacher's wrath at school. Better to suck it up and, in fine Irish tradition, seek revenge. It didn't take us long at all to hatch a simple but deeply gratifying plot.

Mr. Mullen, we knew, rode his bicycle each day along the same narrow, hilly lanes to and from the schoolhouse. All we had to do was wait for a decent cold snap, and when the weather conspired with us, we scoped out the ideal spot in the road to ambush our enemy. Settling on a nice curve with a steep slope that veered off into a thicket of thornbushes, we proceeded to douse the road with the buckets of water we'd brought for the occasion. The water quickly froze into a sheet of black ice, and we scurried behind a snowy hedge to watch and wait. Sure enough, along came Mr. Mullen like the Wicked Witch of the West on his big black bike, feet strapped to the pedals, his school satchel resting in the straw basket affixed to the bike's handlebars. We could barely contain our excited giggles as he hit the ice and went down with a thud, slipping and sliding, feet still strapped to the pedals, straight into the prickle bushes. As an added bonus, his satchel went flying, too, scattering our classwork into the slush and snow. We hightailed it out of there without a backward glance. As further proof that God was on our side in the undeclared war against Mr. Mullen, Mick also managed at some point to steal the teacher's strap, and it wasn't replaced.

While we were on holiday in Ireland, I would take John and Caroline on long walks through the green countryside, and they would delight in the sheep ranging free in the hills around us. I explained how the different-colored x's painted on their backs helped identify which farmer they belonged to.

Caroline was a true nature girl, with a deep compassion for all living things, animals in particular. She had gotten up with her mother at dawn to ride to the hounds before, but I'm certain Madam and her fellow equestriennes had held back on those days, because Caroline would never have been able to stomach the thought of a fox being killed. I didn't even realize what was happening myself until Madam came in one afternoon from the stables aglow with excitement. "We did good today," she told me. "We got a fox." I had heard the hounds making a bloodcurdling racket up in the hills earlier, and now I understood why.

John shared his sister's love of animals but had failed to measure up to Caroline's gold standard of compassion more than once, and felt her wrath. One of John's favorite toys was that big semi-truck he used to roll noisily down the hallway at the crack of dawn in hopes of rousing Maud Shaw, me, or the cook to come keep him company. It opened and closed like a garage in the back, and John often shut his guinea pig inside to give it joy rides, the joy being likely more John's than the guinea pig's. One day he took a break from playing to wander into the kitchen for a midafternoon snack. He parked his truck by the back elevator and forgot all about it. The next morning, when he went to get his guinea pig out of its cage and discovered it empty, he raced to me in tears. We went and found the truck.

The guinea pig was alive, but wobbly. Caroline pounced on her forgetful brother.

"How could you do such a horrible thing, John? That's so cruel!" she cried. "You almost killed him!"

"I didn't mean to!" John wailed.

The guinea pig was revived with food and water, and he lived to ride again.

Caroline wasn't the only one who had issues with John's care of pets, though mine had nothing to do with neglect.

John kept a two-foot snake in a terrarium in his room. I hate snakes and wouldn't touch the thing no matter how many times he promised me it was perfectly nice and wouldn't bite. He liked to wear the snake draped around his neck. The super knew about the pet reptile and had warned John to always close his toilet lid and keep the snake away from open spaces inside the apartment. Madam had no problems with a reptile in residence, but caring for it was entirely John's responsibility, same as Caroline with her pretty little parakeets.

"Kat, can we please go to the pet store to get a mouse for my snake?" John asked me one day. Visiting the neighborhood pet shop was always a fun outing, so off we went. John used his allowance to pay for a sweet little white mouse and carried him home in a sandwich bag. That should have been a clue of what was to come, but I missed it. I had some vague notion that we were buying a friend to keep the snake company.

Back at the apartment, we went to John's room to put the mouse in its new home, or so I thought.

"You want to see this?" John asked me.

"What?" I asked innocently.

"Watch this."

He set the mouse inside the terrarium. Around and around it ran with the snake coiled in its corner until quick as lightning it struck, swallowing the terrified mouse one, two, three. I flew out of the room before the small bulge made its way down the length of the snake. I thought it was the cruelest thing I'd ever seen. I still had to occasionally accompany John to the pet store to buy a mouse, but we had an unspoken understanding not to discuss its fate.

There was a wooden cover over the top of the snake's terrarium, but either John was careless or the snake was stronger than we thought, because it still somehow managed to get out one time. We searched everywhere—behind curtains, in potted plants, under the cook's bed—and tried to keep quiet about what we were looking for. No sense inciting panic, and John was certain he could find the snake and skirt getting in trouble for losing it. I don't know which was more terrifying for me—finding it, or not finding it. John was notorious for misplacing things—he went through at least three school blazers a year—and repeated scolding from his mother never did do much to break the pattern. The snake was nowhere to be found.

A few days later, the super called to ask if John's snake was missing. A woman on the tenth floor had just found one in the worst possible way when she sat on her toilet. One of the Secret Service men went to retrieve the snake and deliver a handwritten note of apology from Madam.

What I would've given to read that one.

We got in lots of sightseeing when we weren't just enjoying the life of leisure on our borrowed estate. Ireland afforded the kids and Madam a kind of privacy they never enjoyed back home. There were no paparazzi hounding them, just occasional news photographers keeping a respectful distance when we went to church or on special VIP tours, like the one where we got to watch artisans blow glass at the Waterford factory. Madam was presented with a big crystal bowl etched with an image of PT-109, the patrol-torpedo boat her husband had heroically commanded as a navy lieutenant during World War II.

The best time of all, though, was the least fancy, and the most genuinely Irish experience the Americans could possibly have had: the night we all went to a local pub to hear some music and have a bite. We sat at a big table in the middle, with extra chairs and tables pushed alongside to make room for all of us. The surprised regulars raised their glasses or offered a friendly nod as we squeezed by, but no one treated Madam any differently than she would have been if she were one of the local fishermen's wives. There was a terrific band playing that night, and the mood was lively and festive. Soon people were singing along, and the kids were out on the floor dancing. When the musicians struck up a traditional Celtic folk song called "Black Velvet Band," I glanced over and saw Madam smiling as she swayed along to the chorus:

Her eyes they shone like diamonds
I thought her the queen of the land
And her hair, it hung over her shoulder
Tied up with a black velvet band.

The melody stuck with her, because she later asked me about it.

"Do you think you could get me a copy of it, Kath?" she wondered. I promised to find her a cassette before we left. I could look for it in Inniskeen when I went home.

We'd been in Ireland for three weeks before I was able to peel off for a promised weekend to go see my family. Overhearing me make my plans with Madam, John immediately piped up.

"Can I go with Kat?" he asked. "I want to see her farm!"

"That would be fine with me," Madam said, "but it's up to Kathy." I felt my stomach clench with dread. John looked at me expectantly. I knew he was excited, and I hated myself for not feeling the same way.

I couldn't let him see where I came from.

"Oh, John, I wish that were possible, I'd love to bring you, but I can't. There's no room for you. Maybe another time. I have to go up there first to check it out," I improvised. Madam undoubtedly knew I was from humble roots, yet she surely wasn't grasping the reality of that—no indoor plumbing or electricity, a cold concrete floor, the president's son going to the bathroom in a dark shed with newspaper instead of toilet paper.

And where was I supposed to put the Secret Service—in with the cows?

But my emotions were more complicated than pride alone.

That Ireland, my Ireland, belonged to me. It was a piece of me I wasn't willing to give away, a self that belonged only to me and would never be "Jackie's girl."

The Secret Service gave me a ride to the train station, and I spent three hours getting to Dublin, where Mam and Packy were waiting in a borrowed car to drive the rest of the way to Inniskeen. Just getting home ate up much of my first day off. That left me one full day to be with my family, then the last one to get back to Waterford. Madam had promised me a second weekend before we headed back to the States so I would have a little more time.

Inniskeen was of course unchanged, though there was nervous talk of unrest across the nearby border. Though part of the Republic of Ireland, County Monaghan fell into the same province, Ulster, under British rule in the north. The Catholics across the border were protesting discrimination at the hands of the Protestants, and the Irish Republican Army was rumored to be mustering to fight British imperialism.

In my old village, I was greeted like a conquering hero; even the boys who never asked me to dance on Friday nights were suddenly courtly. Mrs. Quinn, who ran the folk museum in a former church, invited me to tea.

"Oh, Kathy, do you think you could get me a little something of Mrs. Kennedy's, maybe a scarf or an old pocketbook she's not using?" she implored. The museum featured exhibits about blacksmithing and the art of making poitin, which was Irish moonshine. And, of course, there was plenty about Patrick Kavanagh, the modern poet who was born in Inniskeen and was our claim to literary fame. I assumed the intention was to display Madam's pilfered pocketbooks in that section, not the whiskey wing, but Mrs. Quinn was going to have to find another middleman.

"I don't think I can do that," I told her.

"What about a handkerchief?" she pressed.

I shrugged apologetically and shook my head.

I lapped up all the attention, but it felt so strange to be coming home as one of "the Yanks." That's what we always called the ones who emigrated to the States, and it was said with a mixture of envy and resentment. I remembered how excited my brothers and sisters and I were when Aunt Rose and Uncle Pat came to visit on Uncle Pat's first trip back to Ireland in thirty years. Mam and Dad had scrimped and saved to lay on a welcome feast. There was a ham and a turkey both, plus sausages and cheese, and cakes and puddings. Before the guests arrived, Mam sent Packy to get a platter from the china cupboard where she kept her few precious pieces. Packy tried to climb it to reach a high shelf and before we knew it there was a terrible crash as the cupboard tipped over and broke everything to pieces. Packy escaped injury but ran out to hide in the fields so Dad wouldn't beat him. I found him as dark fell and told him it was safe to come back. None of us had gotten to eat a thing, of course, since it was all for our guests. We just peeked in through the window with our mouths watering. Now not only was I one of "the Yanks" but I had also come back with a worldwide celebrity, no less. All I wanted right then, though, was to be back in my world, not hers. I went to find Rose O'Rourke.

"You should've told me you were coming, you could've stayed here!" Rose cried when she saw me at the door of the same house I used to clean. We hugged and made a pot of tea to catch up. Rose was still living at home, cleaning and cooking now for her bachelor brothers. Her forbidden sweetheart, Peter, had been killed right after I left, crushed beneath a tractor that toppled over while he was driving it. Rose never married and spent hours alone at his grave every Sunday. She seemed much older than I remembered, and weary before her time.

My weekend in Inniskeen ended too soon, and Mam was teary when it came time for me to go. She hadn't been herself since Dad died, Aunt Bridge confided. I knew she pined to have her daughters back for good, but the money Briege and I sent home each month was still sorely needed. I promised myself that it would work out happily for everyone once I found a fellow immigrant to marry in New York and bring us back home to build a good life.

Mam and Packy decided to borrow the neighbor's car to drive me back to Waterford so we'd have at least those few extra hours together. We were all in the kitchen back at Woodstown House when Madam surprised us by walking in. She was in her riding clothes.

"Oh, I'm so pleased to meet you!" she said after I'd made the introductions. "Please stay and have something to eat," she added, asking the cook to make us tea. Apologizing for the interruption, she asked if she might borrow me.

"Can you help me with my boots?" she wanted to know.

I followed her to the drawing room for the familiar ritual that often turned comical as she braced herself back against a chair and stuck a leg out for me to straddle backward and pull on one of the tall boots as she resisted, until it finally came off. One time, we had a real struggle with it and she accidentally sent me flying across the room with her muddy footprint on my bum. We had both ended up laughing our heads off, Madam saying how sorry she was all the while.

After they'd finished their sandwiches and cups of tea, I saw Mam and Packy off and promised to come see them in Inniskeen again before returning to America. Week after week, though, Madam kept traveling herself or scheduling events that made it impossible for me to break away from my duties as governess on the trip. We were down to our very last week when I asked again if I could take a few days off to go say good-bye to my mother. "Kath, that's simply not going to be possible," Madam told me, adding that I could come back the following summer on my free yearly ticket.

I sent Mam a telegram saying I was sorry.

There was a fanfare at the airport to see Madam off, and from my plush leather seat in first class, I watched out the plane's tiny window as Ireland, once again, slipped too fast away.

By the time the summer of 1968 arrived, the America we knew was doing the same.

SEVEN

Are They Coming to Get Us Next?

It had been my day off when Mugsy called to tell me Madam needed me back at work right away, and that I should be ready in ten minutes because he was on the way to come get me. He hung up before I could protest. I had been puttering around my little apartment, tidying up and enjoying the luxury of belonging to no one but myself for a day. Was that too much to ask? I was working my twinge of annoyance into a full-fledged grudge when the doorbell buzzed and I peered at Mugsy's face through the peephole.

"Don't you have a television?" he demanded the second I opened the door. "No, as a matter of fact, I do not," I replied tartly before catching Mugsy's troubled look.

"What's going on?" I asked.

"Senator Kennedy was shot!"

How could he be shot? I thought dumbly, my mind unable to find traction on a thought so awful. It was the first week of June, we would all be back at the Cape soon, Bobby at the center of it all. Bobby was supposed to be laughing beneath a scrum of kids piling atop him on the lawn, or making everyone don Irish sweaters to go hear the Clancy Brothers perform at the Melody Tent in Hyannis. He was supposed to be holding court at his annual clambake for big political donors. Bobby Kennedy was supposed to follow in his brother's footsteps as president, not as a martyr.

"She said to tell you to pack a bag," Mugsy told me now.

For the funeral, I understood. The only black dress I had was a plain cotton one, like a uniform, really, but it would have to do. I put it in my old suitcase and followed Mugsy to the car.

Outside 1040, the sidewalk was already teeming with curious bystanders and journalists jockeying for position. Mugsy expertly elbowed us both through the throng, ignoring the shouts of reporters hoping to shove a microphone into the face of any family member or friend heading upstairs to pay respects.

Inside, Madam greeted me with a puffy face and swollen eyes.

"Will you go talk to John and Caroline?" she immediately asked, her voice a torn whisper. "Their uncle passed away." She avoided speaking aloud the ugly words—*shot, killed, murdered, assassinated*—that already had nearly destroyed her not five years before.

"I'm so very sorry, Madam," I murmured, uncertain what else I could say.

"I know, I know," she said bitterly. "Same story all over again."

She looked at me with such sad resignation before saying the two sentences that she would repeat over and over to grieving friends and admirers in the coming days. "We'll all miss him dearly. He was a second father to my children."

I knew Madam was counting on me to fill in for her while she prepared with the gathering family members and advisers for the difficult days ahead. She would be hosting a big buffet at 1040 for everyone the evening before the funeral. I found John and Caroline both crying in John's room.

"Your Uncle Bobby is up in heaven looking down on you two," I tried to console them, sadly realizing they had undoubtedly heard these same words after losing their father. "He'll always take care of you."

"Let's go choose a dress for you to wear," I suggested gently to Caroline. She knew without asking that I meant for the funeral. Obediently, she got up to lead me across the hall to her bedroom closet, where she picked out a pale-blue frock, one of the English ones with puffed sleeves and smocking that I knew she hated but her mother loved.

Back in John's room, we found long shorts with braces and a white Peter Pan shirt. People were coming and going in the apartment, the phone and doorbell both ringing nonstop, but everything seemed muffled, as if sorrow had settled in like a fog.

I thought back to our magical summer just a year before in Ireland, when life had felt light as a birthday balloon. John and Caroline always adored hearing stories about Ireland, and I searched my memory for a fresh one to tell them now. I knew there was nothing I could say to make their hurt go away, but maybe I could offer some wee distraction, just for a while. Maybe I would tell them the story of my own uncle.

Dan was famous, but a strange fellow if ever you saw one. The story went like this:

He was my father's uncle, actually, and I only remembered him being old, gimpy, and toothless. He lived by himself in a small house with a slate roof, so far into the fields that you couldn't even get there by bicycle, just on foot. The path was too narrow and overgrown for even a horse and cart.

Dan would come to our house every night for a supper of thick porridge with milk my mam fixed for him. He would rap on the door with his walking stick, then duck around the corner to hide on us when we opened it, but of course we always knew who it was. He never came inside, preferring to take his tin cup full of the hot, pasty gruel and eat it while sitting on a large stone in the yard. He would tell us stories and sing us songs in Gaelic, and I had no idea what he was talking about. We had to study Gaelic in school, but it's a very difficult language to learn, and quite tricky to pronounce. Dan had a gift for it, though, and he was known far and wide for his unusual mastery of it. Professors and scholars and reporters wanting to interview him had heard of a recluse in Inniskeen who spoke the language perfectly, and they used to track Dan down and trek to his cottage door, in hopes of a meeting or an enlightening evening at the pub. Dan always turned them away. He usually wouldn't even answer their knocks. The visitors would ask my father what Dan liked, then leave little gifts on his stoop, hoping a bottle of whiskey or pouch of tobacco would soften him up, but Dan never budged.

I remembered one time when I was struggling with some Gaelic homework, growing frustrated with the complicated grammar and old-fashioned Celtic lettering. At my mother's urging, I went to see Dan to ask for help. To my surprise, he readily obliged. Next thing I knew, though, the headmaster was waving my paper with its perfect score in my face, his cheeks flushed rosy with excitement.

"Kathleen, where did you get this?" he demanded.

"A book," I lied.

"No, you didn't! You got it off your uncle, I know it! I've tried to speak with him, but he wouldn't see me!"

All these smart men assumed Dan considered them beneath his bother, unworthy keepers of our dying language. Or maybe he was just a mad hermit. I think the truth is that he just avoided everyone out of embarrassment. His clothes were old and raggedy, and when Dad gave him a nice shirt from our care packages from Aunt Rose and Uncle Pat in America, Dan would put on the clean shirt and then put his old dirty one on over it, to save the newer one. He didn't have a proper jacket to wear out to supper or to the pub, and there wasn't much he could eat anyway, toothless as he was. He stayed in because that was easiest, is all.

I didn't tell the grieving Kennedy children how Dan had suffered a heart attack when I was around twelve, that the ambulance had to wait up on the lane while my father and Packy carried him through the fields, with me holding Dan's head up so it didn't drop. I saw his lips suddenly turn blue, and Dad told us to set him down. Uncle Dan died before the medics could even reach him. When you're just a child, the image of death stays with you in a more powerful way than when you're an adult who's had a lifetime already to ponder it.

That's why I remembered the silence after Dan's last breath more vividly than the melody of his lost language.

More than two thousand mourners had filled St. Patrick's Cathedral for Bobby's requiem Mass, including President and Mrs. Lyndon B. Johnson, and Hollywood stars like Cary Grant and Shirley MacLaine, who had considered him a close friend. Leonard Bernstein conducted the symphony orchestra, and Andy Williams sang a heart-wrenching "Battle Hymn of the Republic," one of Bobby's favorite ballads. From my seat with the rest of the Kennedy help in the middle of the vast cathedral, I searched out the familiar silhouettes of Madam and the children in a front pew with the rest of the family. As I listened to Teddy eulogize his last brother as "a good and decent man, who saw wrong and tried to right it," I felt my heart fill with deep pride that I had known such a man, and sorrow that we all had lost him now. When the service was over, we filed out of the cool, dark cathedral and into the humid noon to follow the hearse to the train that would carry Bobby's coffin to Washington.

I met up with Madam and the children on board in the car reserved for the family, and hurried to get John and Caroline settled as the train lurched out of Penn Station into the sunlight of a joyless spring day. I made sure to keep an eagle eye on seven-year-old John; he was more wound up than usual from the past few days, and I knew how hard it must have been for him to stay still during the long church service. ("Be sure to take a change of clothes for the children, Kath," Madam had reminded me as I packed everyone up that morning, "especially John.") They would need to be presentable when we arrived in Washington. Did I know, she wondered, where her black veil was?)

As we got under way, John quickly latched on to his best buddy, William Kennedy Smith, and the two cousins were soon crawling around on the floor with their toy cars. True to form, John was a mess even before waiters came through the train with the trays of sandwiches and soft drinks for us. They offered baskets with coloring books, games, and cards to the children. "Wouldn't you like to play some checkers now?" I cajoled the boys. "Or a hand of Old Maid?" I glanced over at Caroline, wishing she could be distracted as easily. *No ten-year-old should be so used to this*, I thought helplessly. Caroline, too, had sought out her closest cousin and best friend. Courtney Kennedy was just eleven herself. As the train rolled through the big cities, small towns, and open fields where mourners lined the tracks by the tens of thousands to bid farewell, the two girls clung to each other and sobbed, Bobby's daughter and John's.

Bobby's casket was in the last car of the funeral train.

There was no way the children could not have seen—and kept on seeing—the image of their beloved uncle on that kitchen floor of the Los Angeles hotel where he had been shot multiple times after winning the Democratic primary in California. The horrifying picture was on the front page of every newspaper and tabloid, and was being shown again and again on television.

Bobby's own twelve-year-old son, David, had witnessed it on

the TV alone in his hotel room in LA that night. He had been put to bed and was thought to be sleeping, but he had secretly stayed awake to watch his father's victory speech around midnight. He saw Bobby flash the cheering crowd a peace sign before he left the podium, and he heard the loud gunshots and panicked screams before the news cameras panned to Bobby lying motionless on that kitchen floor as someone cried: "Senator Robert F. Kennedy has been shot!"

In the chaos and confusion that followed, it was hours before anyone thought to go check on David.

He looked like he was still in shock, sitting on the funeral train amid his brothers and cousins but at the same time somewhere far away and by himself.

As the train clacked slowly south, I prayed that Bobby's life, not his death, would create the image that would linger not only for his own children but also for the nieces and nephews who loved him so. I wondered how Madam would get through this, what unbearable anguish her brave face must be masking. I caught a glimpse of her a few seats away, dabbing at tears as her sister murmured words of comfort, and I couldn't help but wonder if she wasn't reliving those horrific moments in the backseat of that limousine in Dallas.

Grandma Rose sat nearby, too, eyes closed as her gnarled fingers moved bead by bead, prayer by prayer, through the rosary she held. There was a priest holding his rosary, too, as he stopped to murmur words of comfort. Caroline and Courtney, joined by their cousins Maria and Sydney, wept together, while Bobby's boys seemed lost in their own hurt silence. The adults mostly got through the awful hours with practiced grace and anguished stone faces. Ethel was threading her way through the train's twenty cars with her oldest son, fifteen-year-old Joe, the two of them bravely determined to personally thank the seven hundred–plus friends and dignitaries who had been invited to accompany the family to the graveside service at Arlington National Cemetery.

Coretta Scott King was aboard, in widow's black, mere weeks since burying her own assassinated husband. Madam had attended Dr. King's funeral. "They murdered that man for no reason!" she had said as we packed, her gentle voice sharp with anger and distress. I had unpacked her bag from Atlanta only to pack it right back up again with nothing but black clothes.

My mind drifted as the train chugged slowly down the tracks. It felt as if we were at the center of the world that day, yet shielded from it at the same time. I'd had that same sense of distant remove within a Kennedy cocoon the time a massive power outage had doused every light in New York City. From the fifteenth floor of 1040, I'd had no clue of the true chaos below, with nearly a million people trapped underground in subway cars, and National Guardsmen called out to stop looting in the streets. Madam had plenty of candles on reserve for dinner parties, and the apartment was soon softly aglow. The open flames made me nervous, and I kept checking to see where the children were, especially John. I didn't like the idea of a curious, active five-year-old anywhere near a flame. At one point, I was in the kitchen with the cook and waitress when we heard a sharp tapping noise coming from inside the closed pantry. We all jumped, asking each other what it was. "Maybe a rat," someone whispered. The noise came again, louder and more insistent. *If that's a rat, it's gotten into a lot more Yodels than I ever did*, I thought. And not only was it huge, but it had learned to talk as well.

"Please open up!"

Where was the Secret Service when giant, talking rats were demanding to be let in to rob us in the dark or God knows what?

"It's me! Senator Kennedy!"

That, at least, explained the rat's Boston accent. The cook opened the pantry door and there stood Bobby.

"Is everyone all right up here?" he asked.

He had walked up the fifteen flights of stairs in his suit, with just a flashlight beam lighting his way. Madam's apartment took up the entire floor, and it was a weird quirk of 1040's layout that the service door in the hallway led to the inside of the pantry. Bobby had gotten himself locked inside with the Yodels and boxes of Cheerios. That he would go to such lengths to make sure his brother's widow and children were safe and sound was no surprise at all. With his father, Joe, incapacitated by his stroke, and his older brother, the president, now gone, Bobby had stepped into the role of family patriarch and protector.

"You're doing a great job, Kath," Madam said, interrupting my reverie, making one of her periodic checks to see how the children were faring. I had seen her stopping at the seats of other family members, too, leaning in close to ask how they were, if they needed anything. I assumed she had done the same in the other cars she visited on our long, slow journey; she always seemed more keen to give attention than attract it.

Now and then Ethel would go back to the last car to stand outside on the observation deck with her husband's casket, acknowledging the million strangers along the tracks who grieved with her. I could see their faces, too, flicking by like pictures framed in the train's window where I sat with John and Caroline. Factory workers and farmers, people holding signs and waving flags, nuns crossing themselves and soldiers saluting, young girls blowing farewell kisses and tossing flowers. Mothers jostling babies; crippled grandmothers in wheelchairs.

The number of people lining the tracks slowed the train to a crawl. There were more black people than white, it seemed to me. Passing through the stations in larger cities—Newark, Trenton, Philadelphia, then Baltimore—we came to a standstill as crowds surged toward or even stood on the tracks for a better look.

We didn't know at the time, but as we pulled out of Elizabeth, New Jersey, people standing on the tracks for a last glimpse of Bobby's casket failed to hear another train rounding a curve from the opposite direction. Four people were struck, two of them killed.

Darkness fell, and as we crept through another rail yard, there was a sudden flash from a newsman's camera right outside the window where the children sat, and we heard something thud against the train's carriage. John grabbed ahold of me, his eyes frantic with fear.

"Kat, is someone shooting at us?" he cried. "Are they coming to get us next?"

My heart broke that this innocent child, his father and now his uncle both gunned down, had drawn such a logical conclusion. I squeezed his soft hand in mine.

"No, John, we're safe. That was just a camera's flash, and flowers hitting the window," I told him. "They're very sad that your Uncle Bobby was killed, and they're throwing bouquets of flowers to show how much they loved him."

What was supposed to be a four-hour trip to Washington took nearly twice as long. As we neared Union Station, I got John changed into a fresh shirt and his dark funeral suit with its little tie, then retied the bow on the back of Caroline's dress, and straightened the satin ribbon in her hair. Madam left the train with them for the funeral procession to Arlington National Cemetery, where television floodlights and a thousand candles handed out to the mourners lit the burial site.

After watching Bobby laid to his final rest, John and Caroline walked hand in hand with their mother to the eternal flame that flickered nearby, marking the grave of President Kennedy, where they knelt and said good-bye once more.

⁘

The Cape that summer felt quiet and empty. No one took the boats out, and a police officer was posted at the corner around the clock as tourists and well-wishers flocked to the gates to leave notes or wreaths, or to light candles.

Madam was worried about her fatherless nieces and nephews, too anxious to lose herself entirely the way she usually did at the Cape by painting at her easel in the sunroom for hours at a time, or disappearing for the day with Bunny Mellon.

"How can Ethel handle this herself with all these kids, and pregnant with another baby?" she lamented aloud one day as she headed out the door to go find David again. She was spending a lot of quiet time with him, just sitting out on Ethel's porch, clasping his hand or hugging him, trying to ease a pain that never did let go.

Then, on an August morning toward the end of our stay, the mood suddenly shifted with the news that Madam was expecting a houseguest. There was a ripple of excitement across the compound among the help, and one of the summer girls pulled me aside just before the visitor's limousine pulled into the driveway.

"You know you have the richest man in the world coming, don't you?"

EIGHT

Ari and Seamus

The old man who stepped out of the limo was quite short and stout, but with a bearing I found intimidating, even though I was the one looking down at him. There was something hawk-like about Aristotle Onassis, the way his dark, hooded eyes bore right through you. We hadn't been expecting him so early, and Madam was still down at the beach swimming. I met her guest in the driveway and showed him inside while his chauffeur began unloading what seemed like an awful lot of boxes and bags for a short summer visit.

Despite his intense gaze and coarse exterior, Mr. Onassis quickly proved to be a true gentleman; I had expected such a rich, important man to be cold and demanding, but he was friendly to the help, which always says something promising about a person's character. He was also extremely generous. After I took him upstairs to show him his guest quarters, he reached for my hand and pressed a bill into my palm. I quickly tucked the money into my pocket. I wasn't used to being tipped by Madam's friends but wasn't about to refuse the gift, either. I waited until I was by myself to check my pocket, not wanting the rest of the staff to find out Santa Claus was in the house. I nearly whooped for joy when I pulled out a hundred-dollar bill. *I should show him the rest of the rooms*, was my immediate thought.

I went into the kitchen to fetch him a glass of iced tea.

Some of Ethel's and Rose's girls had scurried over to catch a glimpse of the mysterious tycoon or pick up a bit of gossip. *What's he like?* everyone wanted to know. I just shrugged. Letting them wonder what I knew was always more fun than actually telling them. I took the tea to the sunporch, where I had parked Mr. Onassis and invited him to relax until Madam returned. The kids were out, too, having their tennis lessons.

Back in the kitchen, Mr. Onassis's driver was still hauling in the special provisions our guest had brought. Such a strange assortment it was! There were tubs of white cheese in cloudy water, and tins of black stuff that looked like frogs' eggs. There were two cartons of foreign cigarettes, as well as the fat cigars Mr. Onassis favored.

There was nothing remarkable about the visit, and Madam treated him the same as she did any friends who came for a holiday. They relaxed in the living room with after-dinner drinks, then retired to their separate rooms each evening. No whiff of romance in the air. He made an effort to draw in the children, though, asking them to come sit with him for a spell. Caroline always took her time to size someone up before letting them in—she was like her mother that way—and the way to John's heart was to get down on the floor and play with him, not deliver a monologue. They were polite, as always, but didn't seem terribly interested when I caught sight of them in the drawing room, listening to Mr. Onassis talk.

Bobby's death was still fresh, and the void it left in their lives was not a stranger's to fill, no matter how kind or sincere his intentions might have been.

My ongoing struggle to have a life of my own, cleanly and fully separated from Madam's, took a promising turn when I went to an Irish dance at a club in Queens one Friday night. It was the Labor Day weekend, and the place was packed. I spotted a very tall man with thinning dark hair getting rebuffed by a miniskirted girl. *I wouldn't turn him away*, I thought. He was a newcomer; I hadn't seen him at any of the dances before. I was decked out head to foot in full faux-Jackie mode: a gray skinny-ribbed turtleneck sweater over a long button-down suede skirt and tall lace-up leather boots. A medallion on a chain hung around my neck. When the rejected newcomer made his way to me and asked for a dance, I didn't hesitate.

"Sure."

Seamus was younger than his receding hairline made him look; he was a few years younger than I was, in fact. He was a football star from Leitrim, up in the border region, same as Inniskeen. He'd come to the States on a loan to one of the teams in the Irish soccer league here, and would be returning to Ireland the following spring. He seemed gentle and kind, not out to maul a girl the way the other lads were. Seamus was shy and awkward in a charming way. He reminded me of my youngest brother, Owney. I wanted to put weight on him, he was so skinny. We passed each other later when I was coming off the floor with another guy, and he was going on with another girl. "Hi," I said, instantly worrying that I'd seemed too eager.

The next night, I went with friends to another Irish dance, this time clear up in the Bronx. And there he was again. We danced and chatted, and at the end of the evening, Seamus offered me a ride home.

"How?" I asked. Nobody at these working-class dances had a

car or even taxi fare, for that matter. Maybe Seamus meant to give me a subway token?

"My brother and his friend," Seamus replied. "I'm traveling with them."

"Where to?" his brother asked as I climbed into the car. Seamus and I had talked about where we were from in Ireland, but I hadn't breathed a word about what I did for a living in New York, or for whom. My ex-fiancé-for-a-minute, Pat, had shown far too keen an interest in my Kennedy life, even chatting up Caroline for twenty minutes at a time if she happened to pick up the house phone when he called for me. I had often wondered whether it was really me he was attracted to, or the brush with fame that came as part of the package. I made a purposeful decision to keep my job a secret from Seamus. I liked him and wanted him to like me for myself. I also worried about Madam and how she would feel about me bringing someone new across that invisible border between her family and the outside world, no matter if it was just along the edges. The paparazzi and tabloids seemed to be more aggressive than ever, and Bobby's murder had pushed the usual demands for precautions and privacy to the brink of paranoia. Madam had even been quoted in the press saying something about it being time to flee the country if they were shooting Kennedys, because that made her children targets, too. Squeezed in against Seamus in the backseat of his brother's car, something made me take a leap of faith.

"Do you know where 1040 Fifth Avenue is?" I asked his brother.

As we pulled up in front of the familiar green awning, Seamus wanted to know if we could see each other again. I was thrilled and gave him the phone number at the apartment Bridey and I shared, along with complicated instructions:

"You can only call on Thursday night, and you can't call before eight o'clock," I said. The doorman opened the car door for me, and I jumped out and hurried into the lobby before Seamus could ask any questions.

When my day off came round, Madam tied me up with one of her last-minute "do you have a second?" requests as I tried to head out the door, and I missed Seamus's call when he rang my apartment promptly at eight. Fortunately, my sister was there and picked up. I had told her all about the footballer from Leitrim who had taken a fancy to me. There was an awkward silence, then some confused hemming and hawing on the other end. In my determination to remain vague and mysterious, I had neglected to even give poor Seamus my name.

"You're Seamus, aren't you?" Briege said helpfully. "Kathleen's not here, but she's on the way, so call back in half an hour."

He did, and we agreed to meet at a café a few blocks away for a cup of coffee. We ended up staying for two hours. I took the lead in the conversation and asked all the questions. We began seeing each other regularly—or as regular as was possible be-

tween his football schedule and my now secret life with Madam
and her unpredictable needs. I still didn't tell him a thing about
how I earned my living, and he didn't pry, even when a day off got
cut short and the Secret Service came to pick me up and ferry me
back to 1040. The phone was ringing nonstop when I got there,
and I could feel the tension of something unexpected happening,
but no one knew what. *Please don't let it be someone else dying*, I
silently prayed. Madam buzzed me to her bedroom.

"Don't say a word to anyone," she said. "Mr. Onassis and I are
getting married this weekend in Greece. We're leaving for Athens
tomorrow. This has to be kept secret, Kathleen."

I was stunned but quickly offered my congratulations. I
would need to pack quickly—not only for Madam but for the
children as well, since I was doing double-duty again as governess. She stopped me as I set off to get the tissue paper to start
stuffing the sleeves and pant legs of whatever clothes she planned
on taking.

"Could you please do me a favor and go talk to Caroline?"
Madam asked. "I just told her the news, and she's very, very
upset. She's in her room crying."

I knocked gently on Caroline's door and went to sit on her
bed, where she was curled up with her face in the pillow, her
small shoulders heaving with her sobs. I couldn't begin to imagine how she felt. A framed picture of JFK was always on her
nightstand. I knew that however great a hero he was considered

as president, he would always be ten times that hero to Caroline as a father.

"Don't worry about it," I said. "It'll all work out good. He's a nice man." Hollow as the words must have sounded to a despairing ten-year-old, I meant every one. From what little I had seen of Aristotle Onassis, he seemed to genuinely want the children to like him.

"We're going to *Greece*," Caroline answered desperately. She usually enjoyed traveling and I wasn't sure what she meant. Was this it—Madam taking her children and quitting America—or just a wedding trip? It wasn't my place to ask Caroline for more details, if she even had them, or to assure her that she would still have the same friends, the same teachers, the same bedroom, the same life, because I honestly didn't know whether any of that would hold true. Everything seemed to be happening so suddenly, like a record playing too fast to make out the song.

"I know," was all I could say. "Your mom told me to help pack."

Caroline, always the good girl who minded her mother, composed herself and got up to pack for whatever new life was awaiting her now.

"She told me I would need a couple of nice dresses," was all she said. We pulled out some shorts and bathing suits, too, and I went to see about John, who was hanging close to his mother but didn't seem visibly upset by the prospect of getting a stepfather.

It took some doing for John to dislike anyone, and Onassis had shown him only kindness.

"Did you get Caroline calmed down?" Madam wanted to know.

"Yes, she's good," I assured her.

Madam was on the phone all evening long. It would ring again the minute she hung up, and I would catch snippets of the same conversation with each new call: *This weekend, yes . . . We'd love for you to come.* Visitors kept coming and going, too. Ted Kennedy; her sisters-in-law Jean, Pat, and Eunice; her own sister, Lee, who was to be matron of honor. It was hard to tell by Madam's businesslike demeanor whether she was happy. *Is this what she wants?* I couldn't help but wonder. She and Mr. Onassis seemed like friends, not a couple. He was so much older than she was—she had just turned thirty-nine to his sixty-two—and they had nothing obvious in common. I had never seen him go jogging or horseback riding, and couldn't picture him on water skis, either.

Did he love books and art as passionately as she did?

The rest of the staff still had no clue what was going on. "Is there a dinner tonight?" May anxiously demanded as the doorbell kept ringing. Then she spied the suitcases. "Where are you going?" she asked. I batted her away like a frantic bee.

"That's for me to know, and you to find out!" I teased, looking forward to her dismay when she did. Madam had sworn me to secrecy, and I felt proud that she had trusted me with something so big. Discretion was an everyday expectation in my job—I never offered up any details of life at 1040, no matter how curious the Central Park nannies got when they recognized John at the playground. Seamus still didn't even know where I worked, or for whom.

Once I had the children set up and showered, I told them to go see their mom. She was still on the phone, so they sat in the living room and waited until she came in to talk to them, closing the door behind her. Madam came to find me when they were done. It was late, and the kids had gone to bed. I wondered if they'd even gotten supper in all the chaos.

Madam was ready to get her packing done. "And then you'll need to pack for yourself," she added. We would be gone for three weeks.

I was going to Greece? Except for Ireland, I had never traveled abroad with Madam—Provi still served as personal assistant for international trips. I had momentarily forgotten that I was doubling as governess again and was thrown for a real loop by her casual announcement that I was going along. I had been banking on the windfall of free time for myself with the family's unexpected departure, and I was hoping to spend more time with Seamus. That he was more alluring than a Mediterranean holiday was as sure a sign as any that I was falling for him fast, and falling hard. I made a weak stab at staying behind.

"I don't have a coat," I blurted out, as if that would change everything.

"We'll find you one," Madam answered brightly, heading for her closet. She pulled out a gorgeous beige cashmere number and pronounced it mine. I managed a hasty call to Seamus and told him simply that my employer needed me to go on a last-minute trip, and I would get in touch as soon as I got back.

Fewer than twenty-four hours later, I was wearing my new coat as I stepped off the plane—Mr. Onassis owned the entire airline— in Athens. He was waiting there on the tarmac to greet his bride, and I noticed him nervously fingering the blue worry beads he had clutched in his hand. A helicopter was waiting for us and we climbed inside. John was beyond excited, checking out the instrument panels and asking a million questions. Madam and Caroline both seemed cool as cucumbers as we lifted straight up in the air, but I was terrified. The chopper didn't feel anywhere near as solid and steady as an airplane, and when I heard that we were headed for Mr. O's private yacht, I assumed we were going to land in the water. What if the waves toppled the helicopter over? Or we landed too hard and started to sink? I wasn't a strong swimmer. I didn't voice my fears out loud, but the kids could tell I was nervous and kept telling me there was nothing to worry about.

"Don't be afraid, Kat, we're not going to land in the water, we're landing on the boat!" John reassured me. "There's a big space on the deck." I wasn't convinced that would prove any less perilous, but everyone else on board seemed to be enjoying the ride and the view of the turquoise Ionian Sea sparkling beneath us, so I did my best to mimic their devil-may-care nonchalance. Sure enough, as Mr. O's private island of Skorpios came into sight, with *Christina* bobbing gently offshore, the pilot lined us up over the deck of the super yacht and expertly set us down. The yacht's staff was waiting to greet us in their crisp white uniforms. The paparazzi and international press were waiting, too, surrounding the *Christina* in an armada of small boats they had chartered from fishermen and yacht clubs on nearby Greek islands. Madam's big secret was definitely out of the bag. If it surprised her at all, she didn't show it.

Skorpios looked like a page torn out of an Old World fairy tale, with servant women in long black dresses and head scarves busy sweeping and scrubbing the stoops of low-slung little pastel dwellings that I took to be housing for the help. And the help, so swift and silent they were almost invisible, seemed able to anticipate Onassis's every move and every wish, whether up at his hilltop villa on the island or down on the gleaming decks of the *Christina*. No one was ever idle. I never even spotted them taking a break or chatting with one another when Onassis was out. When I went to unpack Madam's bags, one of the Greek girls from the *Christina* was already finishing the task and wanted to come unpack mine as well. I was given a private guesthouse, where the sound of the sea lapping the shore crooned me to sleep beneath linens cool and soft as a mother's hand. I was moved the next day to private quarters on the *Christina*, across from John's and Caroline's rooms. There was a little porthole above my bed, and I could see water slapping and bubbling against the glass. *I'm sleeping underwater*, I realized anxiously.

Before the wedding, the kids and I killed time exploring the huge boat. It was like having a cruise ship to ourselves. There was a swimming pool, whose colorful mosaic floor would rise with the push of a button and turn into a dance floor, and a dining room with a long banquet table where the likes of Frank Sinatra, Winston Churchill, and Marilyn Monroe had been entertained.

Grace Kelly and Prince Rainier had held their wedding reception on board. Had Princess Grace lain on one of the same plush white beach towels emblazoned with a big red O that I did while lounging in the sun?

Did Elizabeth Taylor and Richard Burton sip cocktails at the full bar on the leathery stools—made, or so the crew claimed, from the foreskin of whale penises?

The wedding took place late Sunday afternoon. It was a gray and drizzly day, with a chilly wind off the sea, no trace of the azure skies and balmy sunshine we'd enjoyed since arriving. The Greeks were still all smiles, though, insisting that rain on a wedding day was good luck. I helped the children dress. They were being given the roles that pages usually got in Greek Orthodox ceremonies, each carrying a six-foot-tall candle in the wedding procession. Madam had selected a breathtaking ivory Valentino dress from her closet for the occasion. The skirt skimmed her knees in delicate accordion pleats, and the top was sheathed in beige lace. The dress had long sleeves and a high collar, and she completed the demure look by sweeping her hair back off her face and tying it with a satin ribbon, the way Caroline wore hers. I didn't get to watch the ceremony—there were only forty guests in all, and they barely fit inside the tiny chapel on Skorpios—but I waited outside with the Secret Service men. A few reporters were allowed to squeeze in at the last minute to record the details, and they reported that both bride and groom wore crowns of orange blossoms on their heads, their hands joined together loosely by a long ribbon as a symbol of their union.

When the newlyweds came out of the chapel, everyone tossed rice and sugared almonds at them, the first for luck, the latter for fertility. The wedding party piled into golf carts—Caroline had to sit on her mother's lap—and zipped down to the dock to board the *Christina* for dinner and the reception. Everything was lavish, but at the same time small and low-key. The international press treated it like a royal wedding, though, and whipped itself into a frenzy that never did let up after that.

By the time she returned from her honeymoon cruising the Greek isles, Jackie Kennedy had become Jackie O.

The difference was apparent right off the bat back at 1040, which was now just one of half a dozen homes Mister and Missus bounced between. Madam frequently jetted between New York and Athens. There was a grand apartment in Paris, too, but Mr. Onassis went there alone more often than not. Sometimes they would all board his private jet to meet the *Christina* in Puerto Rico for a weekend cruise around the Caribbean with the kids.

The Kennedy compound on the Cape and Madam's beloved horse-country retreat in Peapack were also still in the mix, though Onassis couldn't stand the country life and avoided the whole equestrian scene like the plague. For John and Caroline, 1040 remained home base until they were old enough for boarding school, but there were longer stretches of time now when their mother wasn't there, and it was just us staff alone with the kids. She called to talk to them every night when she was away, checking up on their schoolwork and activities, but her absences pretty much pinned me to 1040 around the clock. She'd promised she was getting closer to hiring a new governess; we'd just have to make do until then.

One time while Madam was abroad, John fell sick with a bad

case of bronchitis, and arrangements were made for a private nurse to come stay with him—a middle-aged Irishwoman who had won the family's trust by caring for Grandma Rose after her second face-lift. Phyllis was sweet and attentive to John, telling him all about her own little boy, named Robert, and what good friends they could be. After John got better, she'd call to chat me up, wanting to know how John was doing, angling for a visit. I found her too pushy for my own liking, but she managed to convince Nancy Tuckerman to let her take John to a show with her son. They picked him up in a hired Town Car, with John's Secret Service detail following. The next day, I asked John how he'd liked the other boy. It turned out that Robert was years younger than John—barely a kindergartner!

"He kept saying the wrong thing at the restaurant, and his mother would get mad at him," John said. When the nurse called again to suggest she bring Robert over to play, she was politely but firmly discouraged.

Whenever Madam and Onassis alighted at 1040 for a while, the household was thrown into utter chaos. It was like a different weather front moving in, having a man in residence. Once when we were both waiting for the elevator and the doors slid open, I waited for Mr. Onassis to enter first. "After you," he said. I was embarrassed, and felt it would be out of place. "Oh, no, no, you first!" I insisted, thinking it was polite. The doors were about to close, so Onassis heaved an exasperated sigh and just gave me a little shove. Even poor Shannon got his nose out of joint with the new world order: Onassis had given Caroline a white Pekingese puppy she named Daisy, and neither Shannon nor I could stand the nippy little thing. (John's gift had been a red sailboat kept up at the Cape.)

The only bright spot amid all the upheaval was the entourage of extra help Onassis brought with him from the *Christina*'s staff, including his talented chef. Poor Annemarie had gotten herself fired the previous spring after chattering to a gossip columnist about some plan to write a cookbook with her recipes. It somehow got twisted around to rumors of the young German cook planning an insider's juicy tell-all about Madam, and Mrs. Tuckerman brought down the ax with lightning speed. What Annemarie had said didn't really matter in the end anyway; the fact that she had broken the sacred trust and said anything at all was what did her in. She was terribly distraught and wrote a letter of apology to Madam, but that was the end of Annemarie and the Kennedys. She landed on her feet, though, setting up a cooking school and catering business from her kitchen at home, where I dropped by to visit her once or twice on the sly. It was bad enough to lose my favorite coworker, but her replacement made it all the worse: That was when Bea entered the picture. She was as dour as Annemarie was bubbly.

Mr. Onassis followed European time and custom even when in New York, which meant he never wanted dinner served until nine or ten at night. Bea whined on and on about having to stay up working so late. She was more of a cook than a chef anyway, so it felt like more of a rescue mission than an invasion when Onassis resolved the problem by bringing in some of the *Christina*'s kitchen crew. They made everything easier.

Onassis's upside-down days meant sleepless nights for the rest of the household. We could hear him at two and three in the morning shouting in Greek as he ran his businesses by phone with people who were just getting to work and starting their days half a world away. I rarely saw his gray head on the pillow next to hers when I went in to awaken Madam each morning. Onassis usually slept in the guest room that adjoined her bedroom, connected by the master bathroom. Madam didn't try to synchronize her internal clock to that of her night-owl mate. She would still be up as usual by eight to go jogging, and as the hours ticked by, she would eventually go rouse her sleeping husband to let him know she was heading out and make plans to meet up for a late lunch. Mr. Onassis would go to work at his airline's offices in Midtown Manhattan and not get home until eight-thirty or so. When they stayed in, Madam's evenings were now spent having cocktails with him in the living room. The works of art she used to love to regard in different rooms, or at different heights, in fresh light or paired with something new, were all left untouched where she had last hung them.

I had to wonder if she had imagined Onassis doing that with

her, or if she missed the comforting routine. It looked like they were living parallel, but separate, lives.

They didn't seem madly in love to me, but maybe I was just too new at it myself to understand.

Seamus and I had only been dating for three months, but I could feel that our relationship was heading somewhere serious already. We were at my apartment one night when he finally summoned the courage to ask me point-blank who it was I worked for, and what I did.

"Kennedys," I answered. I pointed with a tip of my chin to the small framed photograph I kept on a little table. It was Madam and John on horseback in Ireland. A relative had sent it to me after our summer there.

"You mean Jackie Kennedy?" Seamus asked.

I nodded.

Seamus laughed.

"What's so funny?" I said.

"I'm just glad you're not . . . you know, a working girl!"

I had to laugh, too. I could hardly be insulted when I'd given him so much reason to jump to that conclusion: the men in sunglasses and dark suits with guns beneath their jackets who would appear from nowhere to drive me off in their black cars, this little apartment I only slept in every Thursday, all the last-minute cancellations and unexplained absences, like me telling him I had to go abroad "for my job" for three weeks without notice. (Would it have sounded any better if I had come home and said I was away on a Greek private island and luxury yacht?)

To my relief, Seamus didn't pounce on the truth the way Pat had, digging like a little terrier crazy for a juicy bone. Instead, he backed right off the whole subject of my shadow life with Jackie O. He endeared himself to me even more when he called one Saturday to ask if he could bring his three-year-old niece on our date that day: His sister had a wedding to attend and her babysitter was a no-show. We met at a diner for ice cream, and I was even more charmed when I saw what a sweet relationship Seamus had with little Tara, entertaining her with funny stories and coloring with her as we chatted. Seamus may have been intimidating when it came to size and muscle, but he was a genuinely kind and gentle man. *What a great father he'll make someday*, I thought.

It wasn't all smooth sailing, though. I was ready to kick him to the curb when he called one evening to cancel plans to go to one of the Irish dances, claiming he had an infected tooth and his jaw was all swollen and throbbing. Some friends invited me to join them instead, and as I was dancing with one of the guys, who should I spot across the floor dancing with another girl but Seamus McKeon himself. He saw me, too, and caught up with me as the song ended. He'd taken an aspirin or put some whiskey on the tooth and his jaw had healed right up, or so he claimed. "Don't touch me!" I snapped, shrugging his hand off my shoulder. "The person who brought me will be the one to take me home," I added. I was furious. Let him think there was competition, it would serve him right! He called me later to apologize again, and I realized that all I wanted was to teach him a lesson, not lose him. We both knew our single days were over, and I was sure Seamus wouldn't be testing it again.

That summer he followed me to the Cape, renting a room in a boardinghouse each weekend. I casually introduced him as "my boyfriend, Seamus" when he dropped by the compound to say hello one day and Madam surprised us in the kitchen. He became buddies with the Secret Service guys, who liked him so much they offered him free use of an empty bed in one of their hotel rooms. Seamus was glad to move out of the boardinghouse, since the landlady was always banging on his door at night demanding to know if I was in there (I wasn't). It was the first of many summers for Seamus at the Cape, but far from a typical one. There was a tense mood hanging over the compound, and the press was swarming outside the gates like hungry locusts. It wasn't just Jackie O they were after, though. Teddy was in their crosshairs now, under a cloud of suspicion after the terrible death of a young woman who had once worked on Bobby's campaign staff.

I didn't know Mary Jo Kopechne, but she was one of the bright-eyed young people who were perpetually in the orbit of the senators, first Bobby, now Teddy. There had been a reunion party on Chappaquiddick Island off Martha's Vineyard for the girls who had worked the phones for Bobby's campaign, and Teddy later told investigators he had offered Mary Jo a ride to catch her ferry that night. After making a wrong turn onto an unlit road, his car had plunged off a dark, narrow bridge and sunk in a tidal channel. Teddy had freed himself from the driver's seat, but Mary Jo drowned. Teddy didn't report the accident until the next morning. A week later, he pleaded guilty to leaving the scene.

I hated to see the Kennedy family facing yet more tribulation. I felt sorriest for Joan, my favorite of Madam's sisters-in-law. Joan was as nice as she was beautiful, and that was saying a lot, since she could pass for a model with her high cheekbones and wavy blond hair. Now the public that held the Kennedy brothers in such high esteem was vilifying her husband, and questioning the nature of his relationship with the poor girl who died. It seemed like the Kennedy women—Rose, Madam, Ethel, now Joan— were doomed to live out their private tragedies in the glare of the public spotlight, each in turn becoming masters at presenting a brave face when their hearts had to be breaking. What with Jack's widow now remarried and leaving the fold, Bobby gone a year, and the last Kennedy brother now tarnished by scandal, it wasn't a summer of bonfire galas on the beach that year for the clan. I was relieved when it was time to leave for Ireland. I was even more relieved when I got back and learned a new governess had at last been hired. Marta's arrival would surely free up my evenings to go out with Seamus or just hang out with our friends back at my apartment.

Madam had been royally irked when she finally learned of my little bachelorette pad with Bridey a good year or more after we'd first rented it. I hadn't planned on telling her at all, but as I was getting ready to head there one evening after my day's work was done, I chanced to overhear Madam talking with Caroline in the living room.

"Why don't you go ask Kath?" I heard her suggest.

I hurried to the back elevator and frantically mashed the button, hoping I could still make my escape. The door opened just as Caroline's voice wafted down the hall, calling my name.

"I think someone wants you," the elevator man said.

"Just go! Go!" I urged him. The doors slid shut, and I was free, for a few delicious hours, at least.

The next morning, Madam confronted me.

"Where were you last night?" she demanded testily. "Caroline was looking for you!"

"Oh, I went out," I answered vaguely. Arguing that I wasn't on the clock would have been pointless; there wasn't such a thing as "my" time in her world, just her time bestowed on me when it best suited her. I had long ago lost count of the number of week-ends off that had been appropriated without apology or compen-sation. I could feel my resentment rising as she pressed on about my disappearance the night before.

"Well, I don't want you just leaving without coming to me first and telling me where you're going," she said.

"I was going home to my apartment."

"What do you mean, an apartment? With who?"

"With Bridey."

"The Smiths' girl?"

I nodded. If I was going down, so was Bridey.

"But why do you need an apartment?" Madam pressed.

"Just to have a place to relax, and have friends over," I ex-plained. I didn't add that I was tired of having to stay out window-shopping and spending my money eating in diners or buying movie tickets to kill time on my day off, because I knew the sec-ond I walked back through the door at 1040, that time no longer belonged to me. Madam's face softened.

"Oh, but this is your home!" she cried. "You're welcome to bring your friends back here."

And do what? I thought bitterly. *My friends don't want to come here and sit in my little flowered room.*

Madam had no choice but to let the matter drop. I was still sleeping most nights in the pink field of posies anyway. Nothing had really changed for her. I was still Jackie's girl. But I could tell that this glimpse of my ever-so-slight independence had come as a shock. And she wasn't happy about it. Certainty was her security blanket, it was how she kept her big, busy life running smoothly. And certainty required control. She was more possessive than dictatorial, though. People who worked for her tended to stay for years and, like Provi, would then stay on call for years more even after quitting or retiring. Madam took these professional relationships very personally and, more often than not, returned the loyalty we gave her tenfold.

The new governess, Marta, proved a delightful breath of fresh air. She had spent her childhood in Italy before ending up in France caring for a diplomat's children, and she'd even studied acting in Paris for a while. Right away she got the children busy working on a special Christmas play for their mother. Marta was such a perfect fit that the revolving nanny-door was finally shut for good, which was a great relief for me. Having her in place meant Seamus and I could enjoy a courtship that was as close to normal as I was likely to get. Shopping for a gift that Christmas, I splurged on a gold watch that set me back nearly three paychecks, and had his name engraved on the back. Seamus presented me with a clock radio so I could listen to music on my trip back to Greece with the family over the holidays. Maybe not as romantic a gift as I might have liked, but I couldn't fault him for the practicality, even if all it picked up on the *Christina* was static.

By the following spring, though, Seamus and I were starting to wander into jewelry stores on Madison Avenue to "just look" at engagement rings.

And soon enough, Madam landed on the perfect way to keep a short leash on me that summer in the Cape:

She invited Seamus to move in.

Seamus would come up on his own for a weekend now or a few days at a time, just like the year before, renting a room in town. The more time he spent at the compound, the more quickly he blended into the backstage life of a Kennedy summer, making himself useful wherever he happened to be. Seamus was learning the building trade back in the city. If a drain plugged up or a door hinge or some other small thing needed quick repair, Seamus would often pitch in and get it done—easier than waiting on old Wilmer or his young helper, Arthur, who turned into a bumbling, nervous wreck whenever Madam was around anyway. What really cinched the deal between Seamus and the Kennedys, though, was sports.

While still a teenager in Ireland, Seamus had gotten himself noticed as a rising star in the soccer leagues. He was strong as an ox, thanks to his daily training regimen, and he had earned a reputation for playing hard and taking no prisoners. His iron muscles weren't sculpted in any gym, though: They came from menial labor.

Every day, Seamus would ride his bicycle to work, his office being a mountain in County Leitrim, where he grew up. He would pedal halfway up, then hide his bike in some bushes and climb the rest of the way by foot, lugging a backpack filled with food and water to the peak. There, tons of peat moss lay spread out and drying in the sun. His job was to haul the turf to the side of the dirt road to be loaded onto a wagon drawn by either horse or tractor and taken back down the mountain to be burned as fuel. Turf was the Irish version of coal, used to heat the thousands of homes too old or too poor to have electricity or gas furnaces. Opponents on the soccer field would try to get under Seamus's skin by taunting him about his low-class job on the bog, only to find out the hard way how fierce his pride was.

At the Cape, Seamus had flashbacks to the bog-taunters when he noticed John getting bullied by his older cousins during the free-for-all football games on the lawn. John was still a few years away from the growth spurt that would transform him from scrawny to strapping practically overnight. Until then, John was the easiest one to make or break the family code of honor: *Kennedys don't cry.*

There were always adults as well as kids playing in the football matches—Secret Service men, suck-up Sandy, even former pro football star Roosevelt Grier when he was a houseguest. John had taken a liking to Seamus and asked him to come be on his team one day when a game was starting up. Seamus had never played American football, much less touch football, and had no idea what the rules were, but he agreed to jump in the match anyway.

The teams were always divided into two sides—the Skins and the Shirts. The Skins played bare-chested. Seamus and John were on the Shirts. The Skins, by Seamus's account later, were rife with cheaters who would deny they'd been tagged, even when Seamus presented the forensic evidence: "Look! My hands are clammy with his sweat!" One particular Kennedy teenager kept pretending John had never touched him, which set John to whining. Seamus pulled him aside. "I know, I see what he's doing," Seamus assured him. "Don't worry about it, just keep playing." The cheater was locked into Seamus's radar, though, and the next time he got the ball and took off running, it was Seamus, not John, planted in his path. With no time to put on the brakes, the Skin plowed full bore into Seamus, and both went down hard. The game broke up with the teen, not John, struggling to keep the Kennedy code. Seamus limped back to the house on a twisted ankle. I found him sitting on the counter with his feet in the kitchen sink, which he had filled with cold water in hopes of bringing the swelling down. John was jumping around with excitement over the smackdown.

"Seamus, what do you think you're doing? You can't be sticking your feet in Madam's sink!" I cried. The words had no sooner left my mouth than the kitchen door swung open and Madam herself walked in.

"What's all the excitement?" she asked as Seamus hurried to pull the plug on his foot spa.

"Mum! You should've seen Seamus just now!" John crowed. He proceeded to provide the color commentary of how the avenging Shirt vanquished the enemy Skin, putting on an exaggerated brogue to deliver the closing line over the whimpering cousin:

"I wanted to leave no doubt that you were touched this time!"

We all cracked up at John's comic reenactment. Seamus's ankle was turning purple and looking like an overinflated football itself.

"Let me see," Madam said with the same motherly concern I heard in her voice whenever John or Caroline got a bump or scrape. "Oh, poor thing! He's all black and blue! Get him some ice!" She retrieved a bag of frozen vegetables from the freezer and applied it to Seamus's foot as an ice pack. When she left and I was sure she was out of earshot, I asked Seamus which cousin he'd taken out.

"I don't know his name," he said.

"What'd he look like?" I asked.

"Big hair and big teeth."

"Well, that only describes every one of them," I pointed out.

A few days later, Madam left one of her handwritten notes

for me. This one wasn't asking if there was a dead rat in the pantry, though, or reminding me to make John get his summer reading done. It was telling me that Seamus was welcome to stay at the house whenever he came up to the Cape. It went without saying that she meant in one of the guest rooms, not mine, but there was no need to worry about any hanky-panky. The first time Seamus tapped on my door to wish me good night, he asked if he could have a kiss. I granted permission, but a warning growl from under my bed made it clear that Shannon most definitely had not. If I got up to go to Seamus's room to kiss him good night instead, Shannon would either follow me to growl at him or stay behind in my room and start baying to wake up the whole house.

The carpentry job Seamus had landed that year was on a big project down in the Financial District, where he was on a crew helping build two skyscrapers side by side. The twin towers of the World Trade Center were going to soar 110 stories into the sky, making them among the tallest on Earth. It felt like Seamus and I were on the verge of building something grand, too. It all nearly came crashing down in a single weekend all because Madam wanted to go horseback riding.

We were all back in New York. Onassis was in town, but when the weather turned crisp and the leaves started to turn, it was the countryside and her horses that always beckoned Madam. Fall was high season among the socialites in hunt country, when jodhpurs and a red velvet blazer in Peapack replaced Fifth Avenue and Valentino gowns. Madam was making plans to head to New Jersey with the kids for the weekend, letting her husband stay behind to have 1040 to himself. There'd never been any trouble before with this arrangement, but this time Mr. Onassis insisted that Marta stay behind, too. The reason given was that he was having a luncheon and liked her cooking. Marta was, in fact, a very good amateur cook—she enjoyed puttering around in the kitchen and often watched the *Christina* chefs and sous chefs at work. But Marta was the governess, and the children were going with Madam, so that meant Marta should go with Madam. Hoping to appease her husband, Madam told me to come to Peapack instead, to care for John and Caroline.

"But I'm not the governess," I anxiously reminded her. I was supposed to be off that night, and Seamus had bought us tickets to a Johnny Cash concert. They'd cost him forty dollars apiece.

It didn't matter. Onassis wouldn't budge, and Madam's plans mattered more than mine. Seamus was still on the Trade Center construction site when we left that afternoon, and I couldn't reach him until just a couple of hours before the concert. He was furious. Why hadn't I just said no? Had I even stopped to consider him? We'd been planning this night for a long time, it was too late to get a refund on the tickets, why did I wait until now to tell him? Was it always going to be like this, playing second fiddle to the whims of Jacqueline Kennedy Onassis? That wasn't the way he wanted to live his life, and if it was how I planned to spend the rest of mine, I was going to have to do it without him.

"I'm sorry, I can't help it," I kept blubbering as he ranted on the other end of the phone line. I was beside myself. I'd never heard Seamus so angry. He was dead serious. We were breaking up. Was he expecting me to choose between my livelihood and my love life? I was in an impossible position. I sobbed even louder.

Suddenly Madam was beside me in the hallway, gesturing for me to hand her the phone. Crying and unable to get a word in edgewise with Seamus anyway, I gave it to her.

"Seamus? It's me," she said in her breathiest voice. "Please, it's all my fault. I'm so sorry! It wasn't Kathy's fault at all, she didn't know until the last minute."

I could only imagine how dumbfounded Seamus must have been as he mumbled some polite reassurances and ended the conversation as quickly as he could. He went to the concert alone, the seat next to him empty.

We patched things up, but a line had been drawn—Jackie's girl, or Seamus's?—and sooner or later, I knew, I would have to make a difficult choice. I loved them both, in much different ways, but if I ever wanted to have a family of my own, I would have to loosen the ties to this powerful one that had claimed me six years before.

As 1970 drew to a close and Christmas approached, my sister and girlfriends all began speculating that this was the year I would get the diamond ring. It had to be. I felt a tingle of anticipation and allowed myself to fantasize about Seamus handing me a telltale little square box from the jeweler. I had just turned twenty-six, and if I was ever going to have a husband and family of my own, it had better happen soon.

The box Seamus handed me on Christmas Eve was large and flat. Something bulky and heavy was inside. I pasted a false smile on my face as I unwrapped it. Seamus hovered over me, grinning like the village eejit. He was proud of himself, whatever it was. This was going to be the plastic clock radio all over again, I could feel it. I broke the seal over the delicate tissue paper inside the too-big box and pulled out a raincoat. Not just any raincoat—a gorgeous cream-colored designer raincoat Seamus had seen me try on and fall in love with one afternoon when we were browsing through the racks at Bergdorf Goodman for fun. It was an extravagant gift, and I knew it had cost Seamus dearly. I thanked him, trying my hardest not to burst into tears of disappointment.

"Put it on, let's see," he urged me.

I pulled my arms through the sleeves and looked for the belt to cinch my waist. It wasn't in the box.

"Seamus, didn't it come with a belt?" I asked.

"Oh, right," he said. "The saleslady put it in the pocket so it wouldn't get lost."

The coat was so stiff and heavy, I hadn't even felt it. I pulled out the belt, rolled up in a tight ball. It unfurled to reveal a tiny square box at its core.

Inside was my engagement ring.

NINE

Madam's RSVP

Who'd marry you? I feel sorry for him!"

Not even vinegary old Bea could burst my bubble as everyone gathered round to admire the diamond flashing from my ring finger. Madam's face had lit up with genuine joy for me when I shared my big news, and of course she said all the right things, but her smile had just as quickly faded as the full impact of me getting married hit her. My position was a live-in job. I'd kept my engagement a secret for a full month at 1040 because I was worried she'd start looking right away for someone to replace me.

233

"Oh, we're going to lose you," she said.

"No, Madam, I'm going to stay working for a couple of years," I said. I was hoping we could work around the full-live-in status.

"I'm so glad," Madam said with obvious relief. "Seamus is a great guy," she added.

Obviously I would be living full-time with my husband once we tied the knot, I explained, not wanting there to be any misunderstanding after the vows were exchanged. Most likely that would be in Queens, where Seamus already had a good-size apartment he had been sharing with his brother and sister, who would be moving on, anyway, by the time we married.

"I hope it's a safe place," Madam said. "How are you going to get back and forth to me, though?"

"Subway," I said. It took about three-quarters of an hour to get from Astoria to the Upper East Side.

"The subway? Isn't that too dangerous?" If she thought fear of commuting was going to keep me in my pink posy room during the workweek when I became a newlywed, she had another think coming.

"Oh, no, I take it all the time," I said. Madam had a little-girl way of charming you into reassuring her, even though, in this case, her concerns were well founded. The subway, truth be told, was not at all safe for a woman to be riding alone at night. Even if you did escape the notice of the purse snatchers and perverts, the cars were still filthy and the stairs leading from the street down to

234

the platforms always reeked of warm piss. I was so determined to flaunt my self-sufficiency, I completely missed the opening to ask my employer—one of the wealthiest women on the planet—for a few measly dollars in carfare to and from work each day. But it wasn't shyness that held me back; it was pride and stubbornness. Mam and Dad had raised all of us to take care of ourselves, to never be beholden to anyone. There had to be a middle ground somewhere, but I was still looking for the map.

My biggest problem, Seamus and Johnny Cash had made clear, wasn't Madam taking advantage of me—it was me encouraging it. I drew a deep breath.

"Of course, I'll need to keep more regular hours once I'm married," I told Madam matter-of-factly.

We both left it at that for the time being.

Baby steps, I thought.

Seamus and I had set a date for November 20, 1971, nearly a year away, but I still felt anxious about planning a wedding around my scattershot days off. My imagined time crunch became all too real when a letter arrived from Inniskeen that April.

Aunt Bridge was worried sick about Mam.

One of you girls better come home, the letter urged. *Your mam won't leave bed and she won't eat.*

Mam had struggled now and then with a bout of the blues for as long as I could remember, even occasionally before Dad died, drawing in on herself for days or maybe a week at a time, but never taking to bed like this. The downward spiral had started after she returned to Ireland from Briege's wedding the year before, according to our aunt. Mam had never been to New York before, and she had a great time seeing all the sights for the month she stayed. Toward the end of her trip, though, I noticed her spirits beginning to sink, and the sadness settled over her so fast and so heavy that I found a psychiatrist around the corner from my apartment and made her go, even though one visit was probably all I would be able to afford. It was worth it to get a professional opinion and advice, though. The doctor confirmed that it was depression, and said Mam would probably be okay once she got home again. She should go see a doctor in Ireland, though. She hadn't, and the cloud hadn't lifted, and now here was Aunt Bridge begging my sister and me for help. Mam wasn't even getting up to go to church anymore.

"Well, I can't go," Briege said, handing the letter back to me. That much was as obvious as her round belly. She was in her last trimester. Even though I knew it was true she couldn't travel so late in her pregnancy, I still resented her free pass. My life, as usual, was going to be the one put on hold. Planning my wedding would have to wait.

I showed Madam the letter and asked if I could take time off to go care for my ailing mother.

"Certainly you can go!" she said. She knew how upsetting this must be for me, she added. Nancy Tuckerman would book a flight for me right away. And there was something else.

"I hope your mother is well enough to travel," Madam said. "I'm giving you a ticket to bring her back with you."

I thanked her, knowing even then that the extra ticket would never be used.

When I arrived at my childhood home, I expected to walk through the door and find Mam perked up by the prospect of seeing me, sitting by the kitchen fire and waiting, maybe even putting a chicken in the pot for a celebratory dinner. The fragrance of the fresh bread she had made that morning would still be lingering in the air. My brothers would come in from working the fields, and we would all have a nice reunion and everything would be fine again.

But the kitchen was empty, and the air was heavy and stale. Peering into her dark bedroom, I could see a figure beneath the white sheets.

"Mam, Aunt Bridge said you're not getting up," I said, my tone more accusatory than pleading. If coaxing could work at this stage, Aunt Bridge already would have succeeded. I needed to be tough, let her know this nonsense was over.

"I can't get up," she replied dully. "I don't know why."

"Come on, I'll help you," I insisted. I got her robe and held it out for her. "Let's go sit by the fire."

"No, I don't want to," she cried. "I hate that kitchen! I don't want to be in there!"

I retreated to make some tea and toast. If she wouldn't get up, maybe I could at least get a bit of food in her. She had always been stout and rosy-cheeked, but now she looked haggard and empty. She was only fifty-six years old! I took the tray in and sat at her bedside, but she left it untouched. I wasn't sure whether it was because she couldn't bring herself to, or simply wouldn't. Part of me still wrestled with the notion that this was all a dramatic ploy for attention. She had never wanted Briege and me to go to America in the first place—that was all Dad's doing—and she never stopping hoping that her daughters would come back home to her. Spending all that time with us in New York had only made her pine that much harder.

Days passed with me making no progress. Waiting her out wasn't going to work. I needed a new strategy.

"We have to do something, Mam," I told her the next day. "How about we go see Aunt Kathleen? Do you think we can do that?" Kathleen Carroll was her sister-in-law, who lived a mile

and a half away. They'd always enjoyed visiting back and forth before. To my surprise and relief, Mam agreed.

"I think I can walk to see her," she said.

I had expected resistance, and wasn't sure whether to trust
this breakthrough. She could just be going through the motions
to get me to stop badgering her. "You're going?" I double-checked.

"Yes!" she said. She roused herself and began to dress. Aunt
Kathleen was thrilled to see us, and we stayed for tea and a good
long chat. Mam and I went back home with me silently congratu-
lating myself for a mission accomplished.

The next morning, she refused to get up again.

I waited until midafternoon, then put on my coat and went
into her room.

"I'm going to leave you here for a little while and go see Mrs.
Kirk," I announced. Mrs. Kirk was a cousin of Mam's and had
been maid of honor at her wedding. They'd been great friends
their whole lives.

"I'll come with you!" Mam flew out of bed and fixed herself
up, and off we went to Mrs. Kirk's. By now, I was convinced that
Mam was making a cod of me. Jim and Owney, the only ones still
living at home, were out working all day and spending their free
time with friends of their own. Jim had a girl he was serious
about. Our house was tucked far back from the road, down an
unpaved lane full of potholes, and you wouldn't see another

human being for a month. There were no other houses in sight. No lights, no voices. With her children grown and her husband gone, Mam was stuck alone much of the time with only the sound of the miserable, constant rain outside to break the silence. Companionship was what she wanted, but that wasn't something I could provide indefinitely. I was just starting to claim my own life now. I hated to see Mam suffering, but at the same time, a part of me also felt like I was being held emotionally hostage.

Every day was a repeat of the same struggle with Mam, and I realized I would never be able to leave Ireland if the two of us stayed locked in this tango. The bicycle messenger had already pedaled up the lane with the first telegram from New York. It was signed "Nancy Tuckerman," but obviously she was just following Madam's instructions:

How is mom doing. Stop. Hope better. Stop. When coming back. Stop.

It had been just two weeks! *Could I not for once put my own family first when they needed me more?* I thought resentfully. I wired back:

Not good. Stop. Need to stay. Stop.

Another week passed, with Mam still showing no inclination to stay out of bed and get back to her normal life. I tried to busy myself by mopping the floor and tidying the cupboards. There were still hens to feed, but Mam had stopped having anything to do with turkeys ages ago. I spent tedious hours sitting by the fire in the kitchen, just thinking and waiting.

"I came all the way from the United States to see you and you still won't come out to talk to me," I called crossly into the dark bedroom. "You just make me sit here by myself."

One afternoon when I went out to pick up groceries at Finnegan's market, I walked back over to Mrs. Kirk's, desperate for advice. Could she come talk to Mam, I asked, see if maybe she could snap her out of it? Mrs. Kirk shook her head sadly. She didn't think people could just decide to stop being depressed. This might be more serious than I realized. "You'd better get her to a doctor, Kathleen," she urged me.

The bicycle messenger arrived with another telegram.

How much longer. Stop.

I started making appointments, dragging Mam from office to office for tests and consultations. Somewhere along the way, I learned of some nuns who ran a nursing home in Dublin for women who'd had nervous breakdowns or were seriously depressed. I got in touch, and they said they could help her.

"No, I'm not going there," Mam declared. "They're just going to abuse me and push me around."

"Mam, they won't," I promised. "It's not like that. They'll

make sure you get up and get dressed, that you get some exercise and good nutrition. You'll go to church every day and get Communion." Mam reluctantly agreed to give it a try.

I'd sent word to Seamus of my plan, and he had gallantly offered to use his own vacation time to fly to Dublin and help me. The telegrams were coming from Nancy Tuckerman every few days now, each more urgent than the last, reminding me I was overdue back home, wanting to know when I was returning. I had to walk a mile and a half to the village each time to reply, a variation each time of the same message.

Need more time. Stop.

Madam probably had convinced herself I wasn't returning at all, that I had my Irish fiancé now, and we were going to make a life for ourselves back in Ireland. It would be time to go to the Cape soon, and she was worried I was abandoning her. Returning to Ireland for good always had been my dream, true enough, but Seamus and I saw that happening in some distant, successful middle-aged future, not right away. We both loved New York, and Seamus saw a more exciting future for himself in construction here than back home. I believed in him, too. We had a real shot at staking a claim on our own piece of the storied American dream now.

I managed to deliver Mam safely to the nuns' care, and they soon reported back that she was starting to come along. They were getting her up each morning to go eat breakfast at the table with the rest of the patients, and taking her for mandatory walks in the garden and to daily prayers. She would need to stay a while longer. It took two weeks, they had cautioned me when she checked in.

Seamus flew into Dublin airport, and the mere sight of him instantly restored me from my own utter weariness. We dashed off to Leitrim to see his family for a couple of days, and stopped to visit Mam when we got back. She adored Seamus and was thrilled to see us.

"I'm coming home with you today!" she said.

"No, Mam," I reminded her. "They said you need to stay another week." Her face sagged with disappointment and, maybe because Seamus was there, shame.

"A lot of patients are worse than me," she sulked. "I'm not that bad at all."

"No," I agreed gently. "You're not bad at all."

I still had the extra ticket Madam had bought me. She couldn't have known that her generosity came with a price tag I could never manage. Looking at my needy, broken mother, I knew I couldn't care for her in New York. American doctors were notoriously leery of uninsured immigrants who never paid, leaving their debts behind when they just turned around and went back home. And psychiatrist bills aside, I couldn't very well quit my job to babysit Mam.

Aunt Bridge wasn't helping my guilt by reminding me every time she saw me that this was my fault, my fault and Briege's. We shouldn't have gone to America and left Mam in the first place, she sniped, and bringing Mam over for Briege's wedding had only served to rub her face in the life she didn't have, with her daughters by her side as they should be.

Mam was back in bed when Seamus and I left for the airport. It was early July, and our wedding was just four months away. I knew it was unlikely Mam would be there, so I reminded her that both Seamus and I would be back the following summer for a nice long visit. It was the best—the most—I had to offer.

It was only after my brother Owney moved her to a small house he bought up on the main road next to Finnegan's shop—a house with no memories of the daughter and husband she had lost—that her sorrow finally lifted.

I was expected at the Cape as soon as I got back. Marta was taking her annual trip home to Europe, so I would be caring for John and Caroline as well as their mother again. Mr. Onassis wasn't coming. I went to my little room, put on my lavender uniform, and resumed my other life.

Caroline was thirteen going on fourteen that summer, just starting to tug at the reins that her mother was reluctant to loosen. Her teenaged cousins had a lot more freedom, and Caroline wanted to be treated the same. She was a straight-A student and a kind, responsible girl. She wasn't likely to join the ones who'd sneak off behind the dunes to drink and party around a little bonfire, their portable stereos blasting the Doors or Beatles or Stones to the backbeat of crashing waves. Their shenanigans were an open secret, and though I didn't drink, I knew there were Irish bunnies and other young staff members who did join them. Sometimes a gang of cousins would just hang out in the basement at Rose's or a rec room at Ethel's, moving all the furniture to create a dance floor. Madam always sent me to fetch Caroline at ten o'clock. I would sit in the dark on the steps by the garage to wait. The other kids loved to tease her by loudly announcing that her governess was waiting for her. Even the youngest of them got to stay out until eleven or midnight, if they had a curfew at all. Caroline would stay inside as long as she could, hoping I'd give up and leave, but I just sat and waited, and finally she would emerge, fuming.

"Why can't I stay?" she'd demand.

"It's your mother making the call, not me," I reminded her. I was as sick of this drill as she was, and I didn't blame her for being so frustrated and embarrassed. Madam picked on her too much, telling her she couldn't get the hippie jeans with hobo patches like all the teenagers were wearing, or that she needed to stay away from the French fries she loved to eat. I'd conspired with her on the jeans, the two of us secretly sewing on colorful patches and using nails to shred them so they'd look worn and frayed. She hid them but wore them whenever her mother wasn't around.

Caroline was getting ready to start boarding school that fall at the Concord Academy, and as I stitched name tags into all her clothes that summer, I hoped she would get the chance to spread her wings a bit, even if she did have to take the Secret Service with her. As she stalked home for her too-early bedtime on yet another summer night when she could be dancing and laughing with her cousins, I decided to do what I rarely did, and confronted Madam as soon as I had the chance.

"I'm not doing this again. I don't like Caroline getting mad at me," I began. "I feel she knows what she's doing. She's a good girl, you know."

Madam was quiet for a moment.

"I think that's right," she allowed. "I'll tell her that her curfew is at ten, and she needs to be home fifteen minutes later."

It wasn't much, but at least it would spare Caroline the humiliation of being walked home like a kindergartner by her nanny. She was ready to start becoming her own person. I couldn't help but wonder how that was supposed to work for her when not just her mother but the whole world wanted to cling so fiercely to the child she once was. More than five years had already passed since her father's assassination; soon it would be ten.

I knew Caroline was excited about me getting married and would be thrilled to come to the wedding, but as Seamus and I made out our guest list, we debated whether to even send Madam an invitation. I couldn't picture her and Mr. Onassis in our budget banquet hall at the Astoria Manor, getting swarmed by our rowdy Irish friends and eating poached chicken breasts, but at the same time, I knew it would hurt her feelings if we didn't at least ask. "She won't come anyway, but out of politeness we should invite her," I said to Seamus, tucking an invitation with response cards for Madam, Mr. Onassis, and the children into an envelope and addressing it.

With the clock ticking down, I still needed to buy a wedding dress. I took the train up to the Bronx on my next day off. I'd seen a bridal shop on Fordham Road while visiting Aunt Rose and Uncle Pat. The salesgirls helped me pull six or seven dresses off the rack to try on, advising me to choose the style I liked best regardless of the fit—it would be altered at no extra charge. I pulled on a satiny ivory gown with just enough beading and a ladylike high collar and long sleeves.

"I'll take it," I instantly decided. I put a deposit down and went to my aunt's house to share the news.

"You did it all by yourself?" Aunt Rose said, sounding dubious. "How do you know it looked good?"

"The shopgirls said so," I told her.

"Well, of course they did!" Aunt Rose cried. "They would sell you anything!"

My sister thought I had been too rash as well. The two of them decided I needed to go back with reinforcements before making my final decision. They returned to the shop with me the next day to have me model my selection. As soon as I came out of the dressing room, they both said they loved it.

"I love it, too," I said. Their honor restored, the salesgirls showed me the headpiece that went with the dress, and shoes to match. They were perfect, so I bought them as well. Alterations on the dress were finished, as promised, a week later. I had just enough money to pay for the whole trousseau.

"Does it have lace on it?" Caroline wanted to know.

"No lace," I told her, "just beads."

Everything was coming together.

"I envy you two starting out, doing it all your way," Madam said wistfully one day. She was hungry to hear all about my plans for setting up house with Seamus. I realized for the first time that she must have felt the same way I had, though on a much grander level, about the magnetic force of the Kennedy family pulling you close. She had famously redecorated and restored the White House, but here she was wondering what it was like to pick out tea towels at Gimbels. To start from scratch and make something wholly your own.

"What's the apartment like?" she wanted to know.

"It's nice and big," I said, "but there's not much furniture left, since Seamus's brother and sister moved out and took their things with them. We did buy a sofa, though." It was the kind of maroon-floral monstrosity considered fashionable in the early 1970s, with a high back and big wings. I regretted it for years. Seamus's brother or sister had left behind a cheap table. Other than the double bed I was leaving behind in my old apartment, I didn't really have any furniture to contribute. If this had been an arranged marriage in some country where a dowry was expected, I'd have ended up being stoned by angry in-laws when all they got were some tea towels my sister sewed.

"Kathy, why don't you and Seamus come down to my storage unit and see what you could use?" Madam offered. She didn't have to ask twice. The unit, it turned out, was more like a warehouse, packed with art, furniture, and all kinds of crates and boxes. She led us through the maze of things she'd even forgotten she had, making a list of what we were getting as she went. It was like winning a TV game show starring our very own host, Jacqueline Onassis.

"Oh, this is nice," she said, selecting an Oriental room divider with delicately embroidered scenes on its four screens. A half-moon armchair wearing a slipcover in pale pink and melon would make a pretty accent in our guest room, but Seamus and I exchanged alarmed side glances when Madam also chose two flowered area rugs, one banana yellow, the other hot pink. ("I'm scared to walk on this," Seamus's uncle Martin later said when he saw the banana one in our living room. "Is it supposed to be a bedspread?") The heavy beige velvet curtains were meant for windows much taller than ours, but Briege could always take them up on her sewing machine. I was too shy to turn anything down or speak up about what types of things might be useful. We didn't want to seem grabby, or spoil the fun Madam seemed to be having setting up her imaginary little starter home.

The big treasure in the hunt turned out to be a bulky solid-wood hi-fi with sliding doors that hid an old black-and-white TV. The console had either belonged to JFK or was one of the many White House pieces that were replicated, with the doubles used by his widow at either the Cape or 1040. It weighed a ton. The old TV still worked but proved too low and too small to watch comfortably from our oversized couch. The stereo speakers, on the other hand, were out of this world. They could blow you into the next room when you cranked up the volume. When we discovered big reels of JFK speeches in one of the cabinets, we were too clueless to appreciate their significance and didn't have the kind of machine needed to listen to them, so we threw them out. The hi-fi was eventually handed down to one of our daughters and her husband, who later donated it to the Salvation Army.

Boxes of pots, pans, cutlery, and wineglasses completed our Jackie O shopping spree, and Madam arranged for everything to be loaded onto a truck and delivered to us. Her thoughtfulness touched me more deeply than she could have known. Mam wasn't going to make it for the wedding, and it felt nice to have Madam's attention and interest in my big new beginning. Her generosity didn't stop there.

"Where are you two going on your honeymoon?" she asked.

"Someplace warm," Seamus daydreamed aloud. I wondered what lottery he'd won and not told me about. At the rate we were burning through our budget, he could scratch tropical paradise off his list unless Coney Island had palm trees and hula girls.

"You should go to Barbados!" Madam exclaimed. "I have a friend there who runs a resort. Let me book it for you as my gift."

We were floored. Nancy Tuckerman swiftly followed through on the offer, making all the arrangements. Everything was being taken care of, from our flights and the gorgeous villa to our meals and even a rented dune buggy to tool around the island.

Meanwhile our RSVPs were pouring in, and even with our free honeymoon and all the things from Madam's warehouse, we were still anxious about being able to afford our own reception. We'd invited 125 guests. In our circle of servants, laborers, street cops, and firemen, the custom was to bring envelopes of cash as a wedding present to pay for your meal at the reception. It may not have won any of us the Nobel Prize for Etiquette, but the tradition allowed us to celebrate with all our friends. It was a gamble whether the cash gifts would cover the catering bill.

I had decided to take off the two weeks leading up to the wedding to finish getting everything ready, and on my last night of work, Mr. Onassis summoned me to the dining room, where the family was finishing dinner together. He handed me a cream envelope with a fresh blue cornflower pressed in the corner. I thanked him and went to put it in my pocket.

"Could you open and read it, please?" he asked.

I tore open the card and started to read but stumbled over the words. I'd never been a great reader, and I couldn't make out his handwriting.

"I'll help you," Caroline offered, getting up from her chair. She took the note and read it aloud. Mr. Onassis was wishing me well, and said he looked forward to meeting the gentleman lucky enough to marry me, and how lucky I was to have a carpenter as a husband, because I would always have a nice home and someone who was handy at fixing things. Did I know Saint Joseph was a carpenter? he went on.

"Do you know what my first job was?" he asked. "I was a busboy cleaning tables. You always have to start from the bottom up to make something of yourself."

There was a check inside the cornflower envelope, too. I was stunned when I saw the amount. It was for one thousand dollars. His generosity blew me away. This was ten times the annual bonus I had always looked forward to from Madam at Christmas-time!

John and Caroline had each written me little notes, too, wishing me a happy wedding.

I was at home opening more RSVPs not long after that night when several fluttered out of one envelope.

"Seamus, they're coming." I was in shock.

"Oh my God, what do we do now?" He knew exactly who "they" were. I fanned out the response cards:

Jacqueline and Aristotle Onassis

John Kennedy

Caroline Kennedy

We decided not to tell anybody. If we did and they didn't show, we'd look like foolish braggarts. And if they were coming, we didn't want word to leak out ahead of time, or the Astoria Manor would get overrun with paparazzi and crowds of looky-loos. Madam had always attracted photographers and people who wanted to catch a glimpse of her, but since marrying Onassis, she couldn't even step out of 1040 to get into a cab without the risk of being mobbed on the sidewalk. She had lost Secret Service protection when she remarried. John and Caroline would keep their Secret Service details until they were sixteen. We'd invited a bunch of them to the wedding—Mugsy, Jack Walsh, and a couple others. The staff from 1040 was invited, too, except for Bea. I did end up confiding about Madam's RSVP to one other guest, the disgraced cook, Annemarie. I had told Madam about Annemarie's private cooking school, and Madam had seemed sincere when she said, "Good for her, I hope she does well." But Annemarie was still too scared to come to the wedding, though she did send a nice Crock-Pot.

When we filled out our seating charts, we left a choice table near ours empty. As the big day drew closer, I kept dodging questions from the hotel's manager about who to put down for that table. I bought time by putting Nancy Tuckerman, Provi and her son Gustavo, plus my cousin John and his wife, Mary, there, but there were still four unassigned seats.

"We need to know what to do about table five," the hotel manager finally insisted a few days before the event.

"Prilly O'Toole and family," I improvised. (Prilly was the secret code name I'd made up for Madam back when I started at 1040. "Prilly's coming," I'd warn my coworkers if they were yukking it up in the kitchen and I knew she was on the move.) One more Irish surname wouldn't draw any attention on our guest list.

The hotel called back the day before the wedding. The manager was freaking out.

"Why are all the Secret Service agents and police here?" he demanded. "What's going on?"

"We don't know," I said.

"They're checking out your reception room," he said.

"You got it all wrong," I insisted. "It's not us."

I told myself the obvious security sweep was just a precaution, that at most Madam would attend the church ceremony in Manhattan, then decide to skip the reception, which was three hours later and a borough away.

Sure enough, she slipped into St. Stephen's the next morning with the children in time to see me walk down the aisle. I spotted her off to the side in a red dress. The pews were filled with familiar faces not only from my life, but also from the separate life I had shared with her for seven years by then. There was even a staff squabble for old times' sake on my way back up the aisle after Seamus and I exchanged vows.

"Kathy! Kathy!" I heard someone hiss loudly on my way down the aisle. I recognized Provi's voice and tried to ignore it. She kept it up until I finally stopped in annoyance.

"What *is* it, Provi?" I said, smiling through clenched teeth as the rest of the church wondered why I had come to a sudden halt.

"Where's your bathtub?" Provi demanded. "I couldn't find the bathtub!"

Bridey and I had loaned her the use of our apartment while she was in town for the wedding. I couldn't believe she was now interrupting my recessional march to ask me such a ridiculous question.

"You had your breakfast on it, Provi!" I snapped back. How hard was it to miss a tub with a piece of plywood over it in the middle of the kitchen? I could have smacked her with my bouquet of yellow Montauk daisies.

At the Astoria Manor, the wedding party lined up outside the reception hall door for our grand entrance as husband and wife. Briege was my matron of honor, with Marta and Bridey serving as bridesmaids in midnight blue velvet gowns. As we swept through the door, the first thing I saw was John standing right in the middle of the room in front of us, jumping up and down and clapping like crazy. Madam stood nearby with Caroline, smiling and applauding with the rest of the guests. She made her way over to hug me and admire my ring. The solitaire Seamus had given me the Christmas before was now surrounded by a sunburst of smaller diamonds. Mr. Onassis wasn't feeling well but sent his good wishes, Madam told us.

I was relieved that my friends and relatives were managing to restrain themselves about the celebrities unexpectedly in their midst. Once the music struck up, though, some brazen eejit went up and asked Madam to dance. We'd foolishly assumed everyone would know better, especially since the groom hadn't done so. Madam tried to beg off, but the guy wouldn't give up, and finally she went out on the floor with him just as the song was ending. When his minute of glory was over, the clod thanked her and then left her on the dance floor. That was how it worked at the Jaeger Haus and the other Irish dance clubs, where there weren't tables to walk a lady back to anyway. Madam walked back to her seat, but Seamus's brother Paddy, figuring the door had been opened now, stepped up to ask her for a dance. She shook her head, and Paddy retreated, but Jack Walsh, sitting at the table of off-duty Secret Service agents, signaled for Madam and clued her in on who Paddy was. She was aghast. "Oh, bring him back!" she said. Paddy got his dance.

I looked across the room to see her smile when I had the band play an Irish song I hoped she knew was for her:

Her eyes they shone like diamonds
I thought her the queen of the land
And her hair, it hung over her shoulder
Tied up with a black velvet band.

She pulled me aside as I table-hopped.

"Kath, I have to get out of here," she apologized. "I don't want to take all the attention. It's your day. I'll wait for the cake."

When she went to the ladies' room to powder her nose, though, another bride happened to be just entering her reception in the banquet room next to ours, and the doors opened as Madam passed by on her way back to our party. Before we knew it, all the guests from the other wedding were jostling one another in the hall and pushing on our door to get a look. Security and the Secret Service held them back. Madam gathered the kids and found us again. There was no staying for cake now.

"Kath, sorry, we have to leave," she said.

I thanked her, my heart full, and let her go.

TEN

Farewell to 1040

S eamus, I soon learned, went into our marriage holding on to a secret.

The night before our wedding, he'd answered a knock on the door and gotten served with an eviction notice. When his elderly landlady had died some months earlier, Seamus had actually negotiated a sweetheart deal to buy the two-family house from her son in California. The day before the papers were to be signed, a missing will was suddenly produced by the distant relative who'd been living in the downstairs unit. Seamus lost out, the building

259

fell into the hands of lawyers, and now the apartment we'd been busily turning into our love nest was going to be put on the market by the trust holding the deed.

The newly married Mr. and Mrs. Seamus McKeon were homeless.

Seamus hadn't wanted to upset me, so he saved the news until we got back from our dream Thanksgiving honeymoon in Barbados.

"What are we going to do?" I said. This was a disastrous way to start newlywed life. Finding an affordable place to rent in New York was practically a blood sport, it was so competitive. Seamus and his siblings had been clever players in the real estate game, though. The first ones to emigrate had found the roomy Astoria apartment, and it had always been shared or passed along to the next brother or sister as needed, keeping the affordable lease in the family for years. We were paying only $125 a month for three bedrooms plus a living room and dining room, which was a steal, even by 1972 standards. It was going to cost us more than twice that to lease even a cramped one-bedroom now.

"We don't need to panic yet," Seamus said. He had done his homework and felt certain that New York's strict tenant laws were on our side. As long as we kept paying our rent on time, he'd learned, the trust couldn't just put us out in ninety days, which is how long the notice gave us to vacate. It wasn't uncommon for eviction fights to drag on for years, and Seamus was adamant: We weren't going to just cave.

"We can look for a place to buy instead of rent," he proposed. "Why put ourselves always at the mercy of some landlord or their crooked lawyers?" He was bitter about the way the rug had been pulled out from under him. "I never want to be a tenant again."

We were both eager to start a family, and the prospect of raising our children-to-be in a house of our own was exciting, I had to admit. I didn't know anything about mortgages, but I trusted Seamus to figure out what to do, and what we could afford. He had a keen interest in real estate, and he was eager to learn as much about the business end as he was learning about the building trade. My paycheck had inched up to around $100 a week, plus the hundred-dollar bonus Madam put in my Christmas card each year. Seamus earned terrific union wages with his carpentry, though, so maybe we could actually swing this. Whenever the trust pressured us for a moving date, Seamus would just say we were looking for a place and would get out when we found one. Meantime, he was religious about writing a check for the rent each month and making a copy.

I had my own little cat-and-mouse game going on, too.

Now that I was married, I timidly told Madam, I was hoping to keep regular hours. Monday through Friday, eight hours a day, and no more weekends in Peapack, I proposed. Summers at the Cape were still okay, though. I knew Seamus would be welcome to come stay with me on weekends. He was as much a fixture at the compound now as the Irish bunnies.

"I could probably let you go at five," Madam allowed.

"I'll still come in early, at eight o'clock," I countered, "but I have to leave at four."

"All right, four p.m.," she agreed, though I could tell she wasn't happy about it. "I'm not going to take it out of your wages," she added.

"That's very sweet of you, Madam," I replied. "I appreciate that." I hoped, but did not dare say, that she likewise appreciated all the overtime she'd saved never reimbursing me for all the canceled weekends and days off I'd had to work over the years. Even my normal workdays generally amounted to at least ten hours, plus another couple later in the evening when she got restless and wanted to reorganize a closet or play art gallery.

Striking our new deal and sticking to it were two different things, though. When my new quitting time approached, Madam would often try to squeeze an extra hour out of me with a last-minute list of "just a few things" she wanted done. They were always tasks that could just as easily have been taken care of earlier in the day, like sending me to the florist to pick up more hyacinths, which she would then of course want immediately repotted, repeating the drill a week or so later when the blooms wilted. I'd finish that, only to have her send me running back out to the newsstand to pick up the gossip sheets she loved to read.

Just when I finally thought I was done and had one foot out the door, she'd buzz me from her bedroom: "I'm going out to dinner tonight, could you get my pocketbook ready?" Before I knew it, it would be five-thirty before I was heading home.

I decided to outfox her by hoarding errands. Anything that needed to be mailed, dropped off, or ordered in some shop or department store could wait until three o'clock, and I just wouldn't come back afterward. I got home to Seamus on time, even early once in a while.

Madam smelled something fishy and would try to catch me out if she happened to be home as my agreed-upon quitting time drew near.

"Is Kat still here?" she would ask May.

"She's long gone." (May was not someone you'd ever want to be arrested with.)

Madam never exploded, but you could see the fire in her eyes and hear the ice in her voice when she was fed up with you.

"Kathleen, I thought we were clear that you would stay until four," she chastised me, "but I come home at three-thirty and you're not here."

"Look at all the chores you have me do, Madam," I objected. "When you wait until the end of the day to tell me you want me to drop something off at Mrs. Mellon's and go to Bloomie's to pick something up for you, that takes time, you know. I have a husband to fix dinner for and laundry I need to do at home."

"Oh, I'm sorry, Kath," she said, relenting. Maybe she hadn't realized what she was doing. Not having me at her constant beck and call was new to her, after all. Her resentment showed when she thought I was rushing and not paying close enough attention to her the closer to four it got.

"You know you got a good deal," she groused. "You should be happy."

We'd carry on as usual and just have another variation of the same disagreement another time. Even if we tested each other's patience on occasion, the bond we had formed over the course of nearly a decade held strong, and in our own ways, we were fiercely protective of one another.

Madam's constant struggles with the paparazzi who hounded her hit a crisis point after she remarried, when the worst of the lot, Ron Galella, stepped up his harassment and then tried to get Mr. Onassis to pay him to stop. The attempted shakedown came in a crude Christmas greeting showing Mr. Onassis dressed as Santa and Galella sitting in his lap getting wads of cash. There was a picture on the other side of John and Madam crossing Fifth Avenue after their most frightening encounter with Galella. When I used to walk John and Caroline to school, Galella would follow us on the sidewalk, shouting at the kids to try to get their attention, even jumping in front of us and blocking our path while he aimed one of the multiple cameras slung around his neck at their faces. He didn't seem to mind how anxious or embarrassed they were made by the spectacle he created; if they looked scared or cross, the photo would fetch him a better price.

Madam had taught them to look down or away, and I followed suit. One day when John was nine, Galella pounced out of the bushes at him as he rode his bike home from Central Park with his mother. The fright caused John to swerve and lose control of his bike; he would have gone off the sidewalk into Fifth Avenue traffic if the Secret Service agent close behind hadn't grabbed him. Galella's shot from that day served as his Christmas greeting.

Galella was reported to bribe doormen to tip him off when Jackie O was at a certain restaurant or club, then hide behind coatracks to wait. He tried unsuccessfully to buy off Caroline's tennis instructor, too. He had some kind of a sixth sense for when Madam was going out—day or night, she couldn't leave 1040 without him waiting right outside to give chase.

When I turned down Madam's bed for the night, it was my habit to always empty her wastebasket into the trash bin in the laundry room. Madam could go through three legal pads a week making lists and jotting notes to the staff. One time I came back into the laundry and saw a new maid pulling one of the discarded notes from the trash and pocketing it.

"No, you can't take that," I told her.

"You threw it away," she argued. It was likely nothing of any importance, but I began tearing up any paper Madam was throwing away and tossing the shreds in a different bin, just to be on the safe side. This newcomer was a young, attractive party girl who liked to stay out late with her new boyfriend, and I figured she wasn't sticking around long-term anyway. She didn't know I was in the hallway one day when she picked up the phone, dialed a number, and murmured three words that made me freeze in my tracks:

"They're leaving now."

I knew Madam and Mr. Onassis were in the elevator on their way out for the evening.

"What're you doing?" I challenged the maid as she hung up the phone. I didn't wait for her answer and instead hurried to the dining room window. I could see photographers lurking across the street. The new hire and I had been friendly, with me even loaning her thirty dollars for the deposit on a fur coat she impulsively decided to buy when we were out shopping together the week before. It was an extravagant purchase on a servant's salary, but I figured the boyfriend was helping out or something. That mystery man, I realized in the hallway, more than likely wore cameras around his neck. The maid all but admitted her betrayal when she narrowed her eyes and regarded me with pure contempt.

"If you tell," she said evenly, "I'll kill you."

I turned heel and left her there. As soon as I saw Madam, I reported what I had overheard. "So that's how he always knows when I'm coming out!" she gasped. Nancy Tuckerman dismissed the girl first thing in the morning. If there had been any sliver of doubt about the spy in our midst, it was erased when Madam took Ron Galella to court to make him keep away from her.

The verdict in her favor cited evidence that Galella had even "romanced a maid" to get information about Mrs. Onassis and her children! Mystery solved.

Seamus and I spent most of our free time as newlyweds house hunting. The ninety-day deadline for our eviction passed with nothing more than repeated queries from the trust about when our moving date would be. Even though Seamus was confident they couldn't legally force us out without going to court, there was always the fear hanging over us that they'd do it illegally, and we'd come home one day to find our big maroon sofa on the curb along with the late president's hi-fi. The money we were setting aside from our wages had to go to getting us a new place—an apartment if not a house—and the trust had to know we would never be able to hire an attorney to fight the eviction if push came to shove. We finally found a cute house in our price range in Sunnyside, a nice working-class neighborhood in Queens. The house had been built in the 1930s and never updated, but Seamus was eager to do the remodeling himself and make it ours. I could picture us raising a family there. There was a little garden, and trees in the backyard. The bank was less enthusiastic than we were when we went to apply for a mortgage. When I told Madam that the loan officer wanted a reference from my employer, she sat right down to write a letter of reference.

One look at who was vouching for my character and confirming my livelihood, and suddenly the bank couldn't wait to loan us the money. Seamus closed on the house while I was in the Cape that summer. He called me from the backyard that night.

"Listen," he said, holding the phone out from his ear. I heard a sound I'd never heard before, like a thousand cards being shuffled at once.

"What is *that*?" I asked.

"It's the sound of home," Seamus replied, a chorus of cicadas in our trees.

We'd been settled for only a few months when I came out of the shower one morning while Seamus was happily working away on his long list of fix-it projects.

"Seamus," I said, "there's a lump on my breast."

He dropped the hammer he was holding, and it clattered to the floor.

"Oh God, no," was all he could say. It was just a small one, I told him, on the side.

We hurried to the doctor the next morning. He told me right away that I would have to have an operation to remove the lump and make sure it wasn't cancer. As soon as I got to work, I told Madam the news. I was terrified.

"Oh, no, no, that doesn't sound right," she said when I repeated what my doctor had said. "I'm going to send you to my doctor."

Her physician examined me and reached a different diagnosis: "This isn't a tumor, it's just a cyst," he said. He prescribed something to get rid of the infection, and the cyst vanished, never to return.

I'd always been blessed with good health, and with me coming from a family of eight kids, and Seamus one of ten, I had no reason to think for an Irish-Catholic minute that getting pregnant was going to take time. Month after month, though, nothing happened. After two years of disappointment, my doctor suggested I try taking vitamin C, and lo and behold, it did the trick! The baby was due at the end of 1974.

I waited until I was starting to show before sharing the news.

"Oh, you'll be leaving me now," was Madam's immediate reaction. The flash of self-pity passed quickly, and Madam was soon clucking over me like a worried mother hen.

"Kath, don't carry that, it's too heavy," she'd warn if she saw me lifting a suitcase or box. She told me to go to Saks Fifth Avenue and pick out whatever I liked for my nursery. I selected a beautiful white crib trimmed with a narrow green band, and a fancy carriage with big fat wheels. As my pregnancy advanced, Madam hired a pleasant older woman to help me and get trained as my replacement. She lasted only a week. She was near sixty, and the job demanded far more than she'd thought; she apologized on her way out.

One of my last chores was also one of the most nostalgic—wrapping and hiding all the Christmas presents Madam had bought. As I tied the ribbons onto finished packages, I imagined doing the same for my own child the next year. I remembered how Charley and I would always get the Christmas tree ready for Madam and the kids to trim, setting out the boxes of decorations and stringing the lights through the tree's boughs. Madam and the children seemed so happy as they drank eggnog and hung the ornaments, Christmas carols playing in the background and a fire crackling in the hearth. I wanted to create those kinds of memories for my family, too.

I was lying in bed at ten o'clock on Christmas Eve when the phone rang. It was Madam.

"Kathy! Where did you put the presents?" She sounded in an awful panic.

"Madam, they're in the back hallway behind the curtains," I told her. It was her own closet they were sitting in. She was acting like I'd sledded down from my mountaintop and pillaged Whoville.

"Well, you should've told someone where they were!" she said.

The baby wasn't due for a couple of weeks, and on New Year's Eve, I still felt up to ringing in 1975. Seamus and I were planning on going to a party his sister was throwing. I had my hair in rollers and was making a nice pot of stew over my kitchen stove when I started having labor pains that afternoon. I called Briege to ask what to do. She urged me to put off going to the hospital as long as I possibly could.

"If you go in too soon, they'll just torture you," she warned. I weathered the contractions for five hours, then took out my curlers and let Seamus take me to the hospital. I had lovely hair going into the delivery room. Clare Maureen McKeon was born fifteen minutes before midnight. I was so wiped out I thought Seamus was coming home from celebrating when he appeared at my bedside with a big smile.

"How was your sister's party?" I asked.

"Kathy, we have a daughter!" he announced. "Did you see the baby?"

He took me to see our firstborn. I had it all now, my own little family snug in our own little house, the future wide open with possibility and promise.

Seamus called 1040 to tell everyone our news, and Madam sent flowers and her congratulations.

She had hired Seamus to oversee some renovations on the Peapack house that winter. She came out on a Thursday in March to check the progress, and they'd bickered over bedroom shutters she wanted taken down, painted, and reinstalled in two days' time. Seamus told her it was impossible. The labor was more involved than she understood, and they wouldn't dry by then anyway. Madam had squared her shoulders and thrust out her chin.

"I could do these myself in five minutes, Seamus," she huffed on her way out the door. Seamus was still painting the shutters Saturday when Nancy Tuckerman called and told him everything was on hold. Aristotle Onassis had just died in a Paris hospital where he was being treated for respiratory trouble.

Madam sounded herself when she called me a month or two after his funeral to see if I would be able to work at the Cape that summer.

"You could bring the baby with you," she suggested, "and just work around her schedule." She made it sound easy. Provi was coming back, too, taking over the kitchen this time as cook. Bridey would be there at Jean Kennedy Smith's, presumably, which would be good fun, plus there was Tom and Regina Kennedy (no relation), a wealthy couple in the neighborhood that

Seamus and I had befriended long ago while the wife was volunteering on Bobby's campaign. I couldn't wait to show Regina the baby.

Clare was an easy little girl, and I knew she'd love all the attention she'd get with so many people around up there. Seamus was working hard but would still be able to come join us for a weekend or two. The extra money would be nice, too. We decided it made sense for me to go up for the season. Clare spent that summer dozing in her carriage on the porch and crawling after the oranges and grapefruit I rolled across the kitchen floor for her, until Provi complained that we were too noisy and kicked us out. My days were busy but not demanding, and it felt good to soak in the happy chaos of another Kennedy summer.

Seamus came up and would make himself useful by taking care of little repairs the aging gardener-caretaker and his nervous young helper hadn't gotten around to, like replacing a rusted-out shower outside or resetting the boiler when the heat wasn't working. Madam sometimes forgot Seamus was in the house, and would come sauntering into the kitchen in a flimsy nightgown. "Seamus! Sorry! Don't look!" she would cry out. Seamus would already have turned around to face the wall.

The battle-scarred cousins imposed special "Seamus Rules" for the football games. You were supposed to wait to the count of ten before you rushed the passer or quarterback, but Seamus, they claimed, had a quick count. "It's my feet that are quick, not my count," Seamus protested, but the Skins were taking no risks. Seamus was given a blocker, and it was none other than Rosey Grier, who was the size of a refrigerator. The only way to get around Rosey was if you were airlifted. Seamus spent a good part of the games pinned to the ground with Rosey's knee in his back. It was all in good fun and nobody got hurt. John had turned into a strong, athletic teenager and was more than capable of holding his own on the lawn by then. Caroline had graduated from high school and was enjoying a grand adventure in London, where she was interning for Sotheby's.

Around seven-thirty one morning, Madam came running to find me in the kitchen, where I was putting the kettle on to boil water for her tea. Clare was in her high chair. I was surprised to see Madam up already.

"Quick, get Seamus!" she cried. "There's a man sleeping in the living room! On the sofa!"

I ran to the bedroom and rousted Seamus from a deep sleep.

"Seamus, come quick! There's a stranger asleep on the couch and Madam wants you to wake him up!"

Seamus jumped out of bed, scrambling to pull on his shorts.

"Why does she want me when there's Secret Service out there with fookin' guns?" he wanted to know.

"Just go! Go!" I gave him a shove, and he sprinted to the living room. A scruffy young man was indeed sound asleep on Madam's sofa. A backpack and weird leather hippie hat were on the floor nearby. Seamus gave the intruder a poke and he startled awake.

"What the fook are you doing here?" Seamus demanded.

"I'm a friend of Caroline's," he answered. "She invited me for the weekend and said I should just wait for her."

"She said that, did she? Well, that's interesting, since she's not even in the country," Seamus retorted. By then, I was having second thoughts about sending my unarmed, half-asleep husband to confront the intruder, and frantically ran back to the phone in the pantry and dialed 9, which was our intercom to the Secret Service trailer. "There's someone in the house!" I cried before slamming down the receiver. The agents appeared just as Seamus was frog-marching the intruder out the patio door. The agents took over and searched the stranger, then bustled him off. They let him go after questioning him. Just a harmless flake, they assured us. Madam had wisely remained locked in her room. Once the coast was clear, she ventured out again, still trembling, she was so scared.

"Oh, Madam, I'm so sorry," I cried. "This won't happen again! I should have been in the living room before you!" I had taken the back stairs down to the kitchen and hadn't passed by the sleeping intruder. Madam wasn't blaming me, but I felt guilty anyway, wanting to have spared her the shock of discovering the stranger in her house.

"Kath, you know, we have to learn to lock the doors at night," she said. We were all too accustomed to the relaxed life at the compound, with everyone walking in and out of one another's houses all the time, and so many people always around, plus the Secret Service trailer just steps away. We routinely left the kitchen door unlocked. I made a point to check it from then on, and all the windows, too.

Seamus adopted a take-no-prisoners attitude after that whole incident. One day while I was feeding the baby, a knock came to the same door the intruder had used, and I called out to Seamus to answer it for me. I heard him open it, then a woman's voice saying, "Who are you?"

"The question is, who are *you*?" Seamus countered in a not-so-nice tone.

Which is when I heard the lady say, "Oh, I am so sorry! I am Eunice Shriver."

Seamus immediately apologized, but that was the last time I asked him to answer the door or the phone when I was too busy. At least he hadn't body-slammed her and claimed it was legal because her sweat was on his hand.

Madam asked us back the following summer, but that was my last one working for her. I was pregnant again.

There was no formal farewell, no send-off cake or any acknowledgment by either of us, but we both knew that I would no longer be Jackie's girl.

ELEVEN

The Hole in the Flower

Our son, Shane, was born in the spring of 1977, and Heather followed a year later. Seamus built a successful career as a contractor, and I enjoyed staying home to take care of our family. Our lives were perfectly ordinary, and we wouldn't have wanted it otherwise. I still called 1040 to chat with Marta and let her know I would be bringing the children into the city for a little visit with Madam. She always wrote a sweet note afterward, thanking me. In 1980, I decided to take the three kids up to the Cape for a little holiday and arranged to stay with our friends Regina and Tom.

I called Madam to see if we could stop in to say hello, and she welcomed us with hugs and smiles, even digging out of storage an old painted wagon John and Caroline used to ride around in for my little ones to play with. She seemed surprised that I had come to Hyannis on my own.

"I had no idea you loved it so much, too, Kath," she said. She had bought secluded beachfront property on Martha's Vineyard and was building a magnificent home there. Her summer base was shifting from Hyannis to the Vineyard, but John and Caroline, off on their own now with college and careers, still liked to visit the compound. Seeing me gave Madam an idea.

"Why don't you bring your family for the summer and stay in the house?" she suggested. We would be the caretakers for the season, and that way the house would always be ready whenever John or Caroline wanted to come. Seamus, she also knew, would ensure that the historic home was well maintained. It was a win-win proposition all around, and every June thereafter, we'd pile the kids, the dog, and all our gear for the summer into our van, bicycles strapped to the roof, and drive up to the Cape.

John came back more frequently than Caroline, but the Cape was where she chose to have her wedding in the summer of 1986. I was touched to receive an invitation. The house would be full, of course, so we stayed at Regina and Tom's. Madam's hairdresser, Mr. Kenneth, and his assistant were there, too, tapped to style the bridal party. We all stayed up having a grand time, laughing and talking. Kenneth had offered to do our hair the next morning if we got up early. He was surprised to hear Regina wasn't invited to the wedding, but insisted on doing her hair, too. Kenneth was shampooing my hair in the kitchen sink when I heard him give a strange little growl. "Oh, you sexy bitch," he said. I was too freaked out to respond. Was this how Madam's shampoos went all those years?

The wedding was gorgeous but not at all stiff and formal, everyone toasting the newlyweds beneath the billowing tent on the beach, old governesses mingling with old Cabinet members. Carly Simon sang, and fireworks lit up the sky. Instead of a little bride and groom, the towering wedding cake was topped with a quirky globe showing all the creatures of the world. I recognized the silver saber Caroline and Ed used to cut it as the same one I had noticed on the hall table that autumn day twenty-two years earlier, when I nervously stepped off the elevator at 1040 for a job interview.

Where were you when it happened, Kath?

Back at Tom and Regina's house, the wedding fireworks apparently traumatized our dog, Max, who scurried under a table in a terrified panic. When the kids had badgered us for a puppy, Seamus and I had found a Shannon look-alike at a pet store to put in a box under the tree one Christmas morning. Tom had gone to coax poor, trembling Max out from his hiding place when the fireworks were over, and Max had bitten Tom on the hand.

Seamus and I returned from Caroline's wedding to see emergency vehicles and flashing lights outside Tom and Regina's house. Tom got a few stitches to close the wound between his thumb and forefinger, and insisted he was fine. We were relieved but still mortified, of course, and insisted on taking our hosts out for dinner at the nicest restaurant in town the following evening. John was staying over at the Cape house and immediately offered to babysit Clare, Heather, and Shane. We'd brought a teen cousin along on the trip to watch them, but the kids were crazy about John, so we left them at the Cape house and headed to dinner in Tom's fancy convertible. We enjoyed a lovely meal and were in great spirits as we cruised back up to the compound gates in the convertible and were met, once again, by the sight of flashing lights in the driveway. This time it was police and fire engines. Seamus jumped out of the car without bothering to open the door.

John and the kids came hurrying up to meet us.

"Kathy, your kids tried to burn down my house!" John exclaimed.

"No we didn't!" Shane shouted. "He left the pan on the stove!"

John laughed and admitted that he'd been making hamburgers and left the pan on the burner when he went to take a shower. The smoke alarm had gone off, but that was it. John had a checkered history of combining showering and cooking;

his attention deficit disorder tended to sabotage that kind of multitasking. We never let him forget the time he had been fresh out of the shower with a towel around his waist when he fired up the grill to make us hamburgers. He'd turned around and lost his towel, causing Seamus to drily remark, "I thought you were making us hamburgers, John, but it looks like we're getting wieners instead."

Seamus summarized the latest burger fiasco with similar Irish humor.

"Well, Kathy," he announced, "our dog bit Tom Kennedy, our kids almost burned down the president's house . . . I'd say it's time we left the Cape!"

Caroline was off and running, building her own life now, and it was John who tended to stay more in touch. A month after Caroline's wedding, I had the strangest bit of news I needed to share with him. No one else would understand how deeply it had shocked me.

"John, you remember that nurse who took care of you when you had bronchitis, the one who made you that stuffed gingerbread man you loved so much?" I asked the next time I saw him. "She pushed her little boy at you to be friends, but he was too young for you. Robert was his name."

"Yeah, yeah," John said. "I remember that! Why?"

"You know who that boy is now?" I asked. John looked puzzled. There was no way he hadn't seen the news—it was all anyone in New York was talking about, and the story had made headlines all over the world.

"Robert Chambers," I told him. The nurse's little boy had grown into the handsome prep-school killer who had strangled a pretty teenager named Jennifer Levin while they had what he termed "rough sex" in Central Park. John shook his head, dumbfounded. There were legions of people inside the Kennedys' world, but countless more who glanced off the edges, and, like the strange intruder at the Cape, you had to wonder sometimes who—or what—you had actually encountered. John had even been the target of a kidnapping plot when he was twelve by a gang of eight Greeks who were arrested before they could carry out their plan to snatch him while he was on Skorpios. The whole affair was kept quiet until decades later when the FBI unsealed the files.

I had been too close to danger myself since leaving the Kennedys.

Without Madam's free ticket each summer, my trips back to Ireland dwindled to every other year, when Seamus and I would return with our children. The Troubles had changed things. I had never felt connected to the struggle, though I would see reports of the latest violence in Belfast on the evening news and hear occasional things from my mother or brothers back in Inniskeen. The British troops on the other side of our stretch of bandit country were now removing their trash by helicopter, Mam said, because the IRA had used a garbage truck as a Trojan horse for a three-hundred-pound bomb in one bloody attack. When Seamus and I visited, we still took our customary shortcut between our two hometowns by crisscrossing twice across the northern border. Staying in the south meant a longer trip on a mountainous route with bad roads. Now, though, we would see big scorch marks where a car had been blown up on the road, or the black ruins of a farmhouse on some hill. We would get stopped along our way at checkpoints manned by British soldiers. One summer we had the three kids in the backseat when we were stopped. There'd been a bombing or something, and the British soldiers were not in a good mood. Seamus rolled down his window as a young soldier approached the driver's side. He looked no more than sixteen. He said something in a Cockney accent Seamus couldn't understand.

"Excuse me?" Seamus said.

The soldier repeated himself, sounding irate, but also like he had a mouthful of marbles.

"Did you get that, Kath?" Seamus asked me.

"No idea," I said.

Seamus turned to the kids in the backseat. "Did any of you understand him?"

"No," they all said. An older officer was standing on the opposite side of the road, and I caught a glimpse of him stifling a grin at Seamus's brash humor and Marble Mouth's growing frustration with the cheeky Irishman.

Sometimes Seamus just couldn't help himself once he got on a roll. He turned back to the waiting soldier.

"Would you mind repeating it again," he asked, "this time in English?"

In a flash, the machine gun the soldier was carrying was pointed against Seamus's temple. A fear like none I had ever known flooded every last cell of my body. I don't know how Seamus managed to keep his own voice so steady and calm.

"Please take the gun away," he said quietly. "I have three children in the back."

The officer who'd been trying not to laugh a second ago came striding up.

"Lower your weapon, soldier," he commanded. The boy obeyed. The officer addressed Seamus:

"He asked where you're coming from and where you're going."

Seamus told him, "Inniskeen to Leitrim."

"Anything in the boot?"

"Our suitcases."

"Open the boot."

"Of course you can open it and take a look," Seamus offered.

"No, you get out and open it." They thought we might be an ambush, a family of radical suicide bombers from the Republic. Me, who'd gone to one march in the Bronx because friends wanted to join the protesters shouting, "IRA, all the way!" I'd stayed away from any political protests after that; they just

weren't my style. I'd had a pen pal in the North when I was growing up. Her name was Theresa, and she would send me comic
books and long letters. I wasn't much of a correspondent. I sent a
short reply once in a while, but Theresa remained devoted for
years and years. I was relieved to cut her loose once I moved to
America. Seamus wasn't an activist, either, but he was more
knowledgeable about the political history. He had explained the
division of Ulster to John one time.

The soldiers cleared us to go on our way, and with our children white-faced in the backseat and Seamus consumed with a
silent fury, we carried on.

My children's summers were defined more by the extended
Kennedy family than by our own Irish clan. The years we spent
vacationing at the Cape compound in Madam's borrowed house
felt in many ways like a rewind of the summers I'd known with
John and Caroline when they were young. Now my kids were
begging to take down the strange animal-globe that had topped
Caroline's wedding cake, so they could study all the weird creatures.

Shane, Heather, and Clare played with the next generation of
Kennedy cousins, and Shane, just like John, had to learn how to
stand up for himself at the mercy of the bigger ones who picked
on him. The worst was one of Ethel's rogue sons, a teenager in-
tent on making Shane cry. The old Kennedy code applied to any
child in their circle, related or not. Shane recounted getting

thrown into the bushes, shoved against the tall hedge, and taken out in one of the little boats, which the older boy then pretended had run out of gas. When all of that didn't work, Shane came home shaken one day to say he had been put out of the boat at the break wall and told to swim back. He was all of eight or nine. Of course, the cousins circled back to get him. Shane still wasn't in tears, but he told me what had happened, and how scary it was. "John got picked on when he was your age, too," I told my son. I didn't have to tell him how that turned out, because John was practically a superhero in his eyes. Save for the teenaged bully, the Kennedys folded my three kids seamlessly into the rollicking, extended summer clan of family, friends, and guests, like the inner-city kids Ethel often hosted.

Teddy Kennedy had fallen into the patriarch role since Bobby's assassination. He wasn't the same presence as Bobby had been at the Cape, beaten down, maybe, by the murders of his two big brothers, then by the Mary Jo Kopechne scandal and the personal and political fallout from that. He and Joan had separated in 1980, and divorced two years later. Much as my enduring image of Bobby was with a football in his hands, Teddy usually appears in my memory with a cocktail in his. One day he came up from the beach and told the kids he'd lost his eyeglasses somewhere in the sand or sea grasses. There would be a prize for whoever found them. My two oldest took off for the beach like they'd been fired from a cannon, and sure enough, they were the ones to come back with the glasses. I found out about all this only after I wondered how it was my children were not only getting themselves ice creams every day at the "Kennedy store," a short walk from the compound, but were also doling them out to an entourage of little cousins. Teddy's prize, it turned out, had been ice cream. He had given the children his credit card and forgot to take it back. They had an open ice-cream tab going and were only too happy to share their windfall with anyone who tagged along on their daily run.

"What do you think you're doing?" I railed at them. "No more!"

"But, Mom," Clare objected, "we found his glasses!"

Grandma Rose was still going strong, but old Joseph P. Kennedy had died the year after Bobby's assassination. Ever since, a new member of the family began appearing at the Cape for a week or so each summer. Rosemary was large and placid, in a wheelchair more often than not, it seemed. A nun would accompany her and serve as her caregiver. When Rosemary was coming, word would be sent from Grandma Rose's house that the swimming pool would be closed for everyone else. She would have the heat turned way up, so the water was like a hot tub, because Rosemary apparently liked it that way. The air inside the glass-roofed pool room would be muggy, with a sharp smell of chlorine. Every day I would see Eunice and Pat or Jean pushing Rosemary's wheelchair around the compound as they took their sister for her daily walk.

She wasn't the only forgotten Kennedy relative I caught a brief glimpse of.

Several years after Madam married Onassis, she came to me one day with a list of things to go buy at Gimbels. Mr. Onassis's chauffeur, George, would take me, she said, and then he would drive me to Long Island to deliver everything to some people there. The list was long, full of bed linens, comforters, towels, and other household items. Mostly things to stay warm.

It took us a few hours to get to the address George had been given. We pulled into an estate of some kind, with a big mansion set deep within an overgrown garden. I scooted through rotting arched trellises sagging with roses that must have been growing there for decades. As we approached the porch, the heady perfume from all the blossoms gave way to the overpowering stench of cat urine. The porch and weedy garden were alive with skinny feral cats. I rang the bell and the door opened a crack. I could see an old woman peering through the chain-lock at George and me.

"Just leave it on the porch," she said, then closed the door.

We did as she asked and retreated. I looked back and saw another woman watching us from an upstairs window. She looked younger than the first, and wore a scarf or piece of cloth tied close to her head, like Amelia Earhart's aviator helmet.

A week or so later, George and I were sent back with pajamas, bathrobes, and groceries for the odd women in the derelict mansion. We brought cat food this time, too. Once again, the big one told us to leave it on the porch. I never saw them again until Seamus was poking around on his computer one day not long ago and happened upon a documentary called *Grey Gardens*, about an eccentric aunt and cousin of Madam's who had been discovered living in squalor at a crumbling Long Island estate.

"My God, that's the place I was with the overgrown roses!" I cried when I saw the pictures. I recognized the images of the old woman and the younger one in the window—mother and daughter, it turned out. Madam had never explained who they were or what had happened, and it was too late to ask now.

⁓

I still saw Madam every so often, and we were in regular contact by phone about the Cape house, but it had probably been a year or more since I'd last seen her when I picked up the newspaper and read that she had cancer. There was a paparazzi shot of her in the park. She looked terribly thin and frail. I immediately dialed 1040. Marta picked up.

It was bad, she told me, and Madam was in the hospital. "But you won't believe who's here!" she added. John came on the line.

"Hi, Kathy," he said. "It's so nice of you to think of my mom." I asked how she was doing, and he told me it didn't look good. "She's very, very ill."

We talked for a few minutes, and I hung up, heartsick. I bought a get-well card and mailed it to her with my prayers.

One of Madam's blue note cards arrived in the mail. On it was a typewritten message thanking me for my lovely card.

"I think of you and Seamus and your children often," it said, "and hope we can all get together before long."

The last two words, handwritten, were her last to me.

Much love.

She died two weeks later. I called Nancy Tuckerman, who told me I could come at two-thirty the next afternoon for the viewing. John was busy on his computer in the dining room but came out to greet us warmly. Caroline was at home with her children; there were three of them now, the oldest the same age she had been when I first met her.

Madam's coffin was in the living room, draped with the floral bedspread she'd had as long as I knew her.

I remembered my first weeks as Jackie's girl, and how I had put that same bedspread away on a high shelf in the linen closet, not noticing it was up against the light.

I found myself looking now for the small hole I had singed in one of the flowers, not quite knowing why I wanted to know if it was still there. Proof of me? Of that bumbling Irish farm girl, dropped so improbably into such a life, such a special life.

The End of Camelot

The stereo was blasting "You Can't Always Get What You Want," a sure sign that John was in the house when Seamus and I walked up the familiar path to the house at the Cape. John had been playing that same Rolling Stones record for a good quarter century—the song was his all-time favorite. How was it even possible that John was now thirty-eight years old? He had called Seamus earlier in the week to ask if Seamus could come give him some advice about renovations on the house. He and his wife, Carolyn, were spending more time there, and the place desperately needed some updating to suit a modern young couple. The big burn mark a hot pan had left on the Formica countertop in the kitchen when John was little had been hidden by a cutting board for decades, and that was just for starters.

"I'll fly you up," John offered.

"No, no, Kathy and I'll just drive up for the weekend," Seamus had said.

I hadn't met Carolyn before, though of course I'd seen pictures of her all over the magazines and tabloids. She was tall and willowy and very pretty, but in a different way from the other girls John had romanced over the years. Carolyn was harder to read, mysterious in a way. Her skin was almost as white and translucent as fine porcelain. She was chic in beige shorts and a short-sleeved black cashmere sweater, with a cardigan tied at her waist. She was holding a fluffy tuxedo cat and kissing him as he shed all over her expensive sweater. She'd just arrived herself, she explained, and she hadn't seen her cat in a whole week.

She and John were about to celebrate their first anniversary, but that cat seemed to be getting more affection than he was.

They'd stolen away to a tiny island in Georgia for the small ceremony to elude the paparazzi, who now pursued her with even more fervor than they had Madam.

Provi was in the kitchen, too, serving as cook for the evening and fixing us a nice fresh fish for dinner. She came to sit with

Carolyn and me out on the porch, and we all chitchatted while John and Seamus were off discussing the work John was contemplating for the house.

"What're they planning to do?" Carolyn asked idly, still cuddling her spoiled cat.

"New windows," Provi answered.

Seamus later told me John had confided how hurt he was by Carolyn's disinterest in the remodeling, which John had tackled with enthusiasm. The challenge of preserving history while refreshing the home wasn't unlike what his mother had famously done for the White House during the family's few years there, though obviously the Cape house was far smaller and far more personal.

"I wish my wife was interested in what I'm doing," John told Seamus. Carolyn never came up to offer her input. "Isn't that strange?" he asked. I found it odd, too. You could tell with one glance at her, even on a lazy weekend at home, that Carolyn had flawless taste and a great sense of style. John and Seamus had worked their way around the windows and were within earshot when Seamus's voice drifted out to the porch.

"I think this would be a great job for Carolyn," he was saying.

"I don't know if that's Carolyn's thing," John could be heard replying. "We'll work on that."

Carolyn roused herself from the porch seat. "I think I better get involved in this," she announced. I had the impression she meant it was time to quash any notion of roping her in, not encourage it. We all headed to the kitchen.

Provi's Dominican roots and high standards made her a fairly decent cook and the absolute queen of daiquiri-making. She insisted on buying the best rum, dozens of fresh limes that had to be squeezed by hand, plus five-pound bags of sugar. She'd make them good and strong—one of Provi's daiquiris, and I'd be loaded. She'd opted for a gin and tonic this particular evening. As she opened the oven door to check on the fish, I saw most of her drink slosh into the roasting pan, and had to wonder if it was anywhere near as potent as her daiquiris. She closed the door again, apparently not noticing the 100-proof marinade.

We sat down to dinner, with John insisting I take the seat at the head of the table, the one that had always been Madam's, back when I was Jackie's girl.

It was the day of Princess Diana's funeral in London, and talk turned to the horrid paparazzi who were accused of causing the accident that killed her. Carolyn, who had seemed shy and reserved until then, opened up. She had gotten into some well-publicized fights with the photographers who chased her as she walked the streets of Manhattan, even kicking one. She felt besieged. John was clearly worried about his high-strung bride.

"Kath, tell Carolyn how Mom used to handle them," he prompted me. Provi jumped in to answer first, but John cut her off.

"No, wait, I want to hear from Kathy," he said.

"When she was up here, she'd leave the gate smiling, give them one good picture, and they'd let her go," I remembered.

"No!" Carolyn nearly shouted. "I hate those bastards! I'd rather just scream and curse at them."

"That's exactly what they want you to do," I argued. "They'll get great pictures."

She described how she had gotten chased down the sidewalk by a wolf pack of photographers, and ducked into a building to escape them. They cornered her by the elevator as she frantically pushed the button.

"They were grunting and groaning and pushing each other. They were almost on top of me," she recounted. "It was just awful. I can't take it!"

John interjected.

"You gotta just take it easy," he insisted. "Relax."

Deemed the Sexiest Man Alive by *People* magazine before he married, John had endured not only the photographers pursuing him, but love-struck female fans as well. He was practically a Beatle. But he had grown up in the fishbowl, and he knew how to navigate it. He didn't go out of his way to be rude to the press, especially now that he was one of them, having founded his own monthly magazine, *George*.

I told Carolyn how Madam perfected the art of not responding to Ron Galella when he stalked her. "She knew if she kept the same blank expression on her face, he wouldn't have a picture to sell," I explained. "They all need something different. That's why they yell things and try to scare you. They want a reaction. They want to get a picture showing you angry or scared."

Galella had trailed the family on their travels as well. In the Cape, he rented a motorboat and came terrifyingly close to Madam while she was swimming one time. Seamus suspected the paparazzi were holing up in a neighboring house, which gave them a view over the compound privacy fence so they could see when Madam was pulling out in the new green BMW she'd bought herself after losing her Secret Service detail and driver. It was her first car, and Seamus had asked her why she hadn't gotten a Mercedes. Weren't they supposed to be the best, after all?

"Oh, Seamus, they're for old people," she'd pouted.

She was flying into Logan Airport in Boston one rainy night and Seamus had agreed to pick her up. As he started to leave and pulled the BMW up to the gate at the compound, it mysteriously opened. Seamus was surprised to see Jim, the guy who rented a nearby house each season, standing there in the pouring rain, holding the gate open for him. Jim came up to the driver's window and was equally surprised to see Seamus, not Madam, behind the wheel. He'd wanted to know where Seamus was going, and Seamus had said he was off to the airport to get Mrs. Onassis. Jim immediately offered to go instead. Seamus's antennae went up.

"No, no, she's expecting me," he said.

"I'll go with you, keep you company!" Jim suggested. Again, Seamus declined politely. The weird incident bothered him the whole way to Logan, and it hit him that he'd seen a light in Jim's attic as he pulled out.

On the drive home from the airport, Madam had been in a chatty mood.

"Seamus, I was with Frank Sinatra last evening, and I never saw anyone put away so much vodka," she volunteered. They talked the rest of the way to Hyannis, and Seamus told Madam about the weird encounter with Jim.

"If you had brought that man with you, I never would've talked to you again, Seamus!" Madam said with an exaggerated shudder. "He gives me the willies."

"He's renting his attic to the paparazzi," Seamus theorized. That could explain the keen interest in Madam's comings and goings. The next morning, I came downstairs with a black wig I'd found stashed in some closet, left over from Halloween or one of the kids' plays or something. I had a pair of Madam's big round sunglasses in my other hand. I found Seamus and Madam in the kitchen and suggested we send Seamus out in disguise to take the paparazzi on a wild goose chase. "Poor Seamus!" Madam laughed.

I recounted the whole tale to John and Carolyn over dinner that night, of paparazzi nesting like raccoons in the neighbor's attic. John was aghast that a friendly neighbor might have betrayed his mom.

"So that's how they always knew when she was going out!" he said.

Carolyn listened, but I doubted I had helped her much. We finished up dinner, and John soothed Provi's ruffled feathers by complimenting her cooking.

"This fish is delicious, Provi," he told her. "The flavors are fantastic." It was true. The gin and all that lime had made it delectable. The Stones were still playing in the background, the volume lower, but the song was the same. It would finish then start again. I knew it was because John had done what he used to do as a boy with that very record player, adjusting a little pin on the arm so the needle set down in the same groove each time. I remembered with a smile how he'd done the same thing with his favorite song as a six-year-old: "The Ballad of the Green Berets." He used to make me march around his room in circles with him, the two of us pretending to be soldiers. He tried to teach me how to salute, but I kept messing up because I was left-handed. "No, Kat, like this!" he would say, demonstrating how a real Marine had taught him how to salute the right way. I wondered if he remembered it was for his father's funeral. What a fine man that little boy had grown up to be. We said our good nights and left.

With John and Carolyn making it their second home, we no

longer moved up to the Cape with our family for the summer, but Seamus gave John fatherly advice about the work he was having done and John would ask for estimates and contractor's bids on his behalf.

"If they see my name, they think they've hit the lottery and the price gets jacked up four times what it should be," John said.

When they last spoke in the summer of 1999, John was eager to get the place in shape before the whole family descended for his cousin Rory's impending wedding.

A few weeks later, Seamus and I were having our coffee at the kitchen table when his golf partner, Jack, called. It was eight o'clock that Saturday morning, the day of Rory's wedding.

"What? No, oh no." Seamus looked across the table at me. "John's plane is missing."

I heard the words, but my mind refused to let them settle and take root. Someone had got something wrong. Seamus turned on the TV and the screen instantly filled with the image of John's handsome face with the words BREAKING NEWS beneath it. The reporter was saying the single-engine plane John was piloting had vanished the night before on a flight from the airport in New Jersey up to the Cape for Rory's wedding. John, Carolyn, and Carolyn's sister, Lauren, were aboard. We left the TV on all day, and sat there waiting and waiting for it to not be true.

I called Marta, working now for Caroline and her family, then

Provi, who was summering at the compound with her son Gustavo. We all told each other it would turn out okay, that John was fine.

"They'll find him," Marta promised me. "They'll find him."

She had to get off the phone, she said. She couldn't hold up the lines. Provi told me she had dinner ready for John and Carolyn the night before, that Gustavo had left John's Jeep for him at the airport earlier so it would be there when he landed. I knew without asking that she would keep the uneaten meal neatly wrapped in the refrigerator, waiting for John to show up and say he was starving, what was there to eat?

The news commentators said the weather had turned after John took off, that visibility approaching the Cape had been poor, the sky too black and hazy for an inexperienced pilot. John hadn't had his license that long and had been sidelined for six weeks. He'd broken his ankle paragliding, and had only gotten the cast off earlier that day. The plan had been to drop Lauren off at Martha's Vineyard, then continue on to Hyannis. He took off shortly after eight-thirty that night, and should have been there at ten.

On Saturday afternoon, the news reported some piece of luggage bearing Lauren's ID had washed up on a beach at Martha's Vineyard. A coast guard admiral delivered a press briefing at the Pentagon, describing all the search efforts under way. They were still very hopeful, he said, that they would find survivors. My imagination concocted innocent little fairy tales to explain the nightmare away.

"You know how John loved pranks," I reminded Seamus. "I bet he pulled a trick and went someplace else, to a beach party or something, but he doesn't want them to know because he promised to go to the wedding." Rory's ceremony had been postponed, of course.

Seamus and I had moved out from Queens when the children were growing up, buying a house a block from the shore in Rocky Point, Long Island. Seamus was sure the flight path John had taken would have had him flying right past our house. The night would have still been clear and beautiful then. He would have been safe with us.

At Mass on Sunday, we prayed with our congregation for the Kennedy family, and for the Bessettes. The priest left prayer cards and red roses at the back of the church to take on our way out. Later that night, the coast guard admiral was back on TV, announcing that they were shifting their focus from search and rescue to search and recovery, official words to say they had given up hope. The admiral went on to say that there was little chance of survival in the cold New England waters past eighteen hours at most.

"He probably survived, Seamus," I said. "You know he's a very good swimmer. He survived and swam to a little island. He loves hanging out in the sea grasses." I pictured John resting there in his sea grass nest until rescuers arrived and found him.

"No, no, no," Seamus tried to tell me. A plane going that speed and with that force—no one could survive that.

We left CNN on around the clock, waking up from each fitful night to more footage of searchers in inflatable boats bobbing in the waves, with coast guard helicopters circling overhead. On Tuesday, the plane was found a hundred feet deep, resting on the ocean floor. On the fifth day, the bodies of John, Carolyn, and Lauren were recovered and cremated. Their ashes were scattered at sea the next morning.

"That's the end of Camelot," I said.

I woke up convinced I had dreamed it all, or maybe blacked out. It didn't happen, none of it. It couldn't happen.

Nancy Tuckerman told us we would need to pick up special passes for John's memorial service at a school off Park Avenue. When I came out, I was flustered by the clamoring mass of journalists now facing me. Cameras and cameras and cameras, and satellite trucks. Seamus and I kept trying to ask people how to get to St. Thomas More, where the service was being held, until finally a cop who seemed to be in charge of crowd control yelled over the noise to a younger one: *Walk them over!* As he escorted us across the street to point us in the right direction, a cameraman suddenly spotted the telltale white envelope we were clutching with passes to the service, and he started clicking away. Two other TV stations chased us down the block and cornered us, then started fighting over whose interview it was. We dodged them both and entered the church.

The service was funny and tender and beautiful, like the little boy I had watched grow up. Jack Walsh was an usher, and across the aisle I recognized one of the McDonnell boys who had gone with us on that trip to Ireland, a grown man now, tears coursing down his face. We ran into Ethel when it was over.

"We lost a good man today," Seamus told her.

"Seamus, we don't know what we lost today," she replied urgently. "We have no idea."

At home that night, I pulled out the scrapbooks where I kept all my old pictures and letters from my life with the Kennedys.

I poured a glass of wine and sat on the sofa as I thumbed through the yellowing pages.

There was John at four, taking a ski lesson while his Secret Service agent and I looked on. Jack Walsh was wearing my borrowed gloves.

There was that note from Madam asking whether the bad smell in the pantry was a dead rat, and one telling me she had bought a souvenir fan for me in Spain.

Here was Caroline's wedding invitation and her handwritten thank-yous for little baby gifts I had sent her when she became a mother. She had sent gifts for my children over the years as well, and her graciousness reminded me so much of her mother. If I brought my children to see her at 1040, Madam could never let us leave without finding some small toy or trinket to give them. She fussed at Marta the time she found us visiting with her in the kitchen. *"Why didn't you tell me Kathy was coming?"* She had gone into the pantry to rummage around on the shelves, triumphantly returning with a large ceramic duck for my kids. It was a big gravy boat, actually, wholly unsuitable as a toy but a fine addition to my Thanksgiving table.

Recently, my granddaughter, Keira, was fascinated by it when I lifted its wings to pour giblet gravy from its back. Where did that come from? she wanted to know.

"From this wonderful woman I used to work for," I said.

"Who was she?"

"I'll tell you the story someday."

My life felt full of tender little clues of that other life I once had. I collected colored glass bottles like Madam used to do when we browsed in antique shops up at the Cape. I kept them on a high window ledge where the sun shot prismed light across my living room. I'd won a prize for best costume at our club's Halloween party when I went as Marge Simpson, and no one guessed that the canary yellow dress I wore with little bows on the shoulders was Jacqueline Kennedy Onassis's hand-me-down nightgown.

The good night prayer I had learned as a child in Ireland and taught my children and then my grandchildren was the same one I had taught John and Caroline as they knelt beside their childhood beds. I prayed for the angels to watch over them still.

I turned the pages of the scrapbook and smiled at the snapshots of Marta and Provi and a waitress named Nora who had gotten her nose fixed in hopes of getting Mr. Onassis to hire her as a stewardess for his airline.

There was a long letter from Madam on Olympic stationery, telling me what John and Caroline could and couldn't do when they arrived home after several weeks in Greece. They could have cousins and friends sleep over at 1040, but no more than four or five, and everyone had to stay out of Madam's room. The children were to play tennis every day.

They wanted to start flying lessons, she wrote me (I knew that a neighbor at the Cape with a plane and a license had offered), but that was not to happen. If John insisted, I was to tell him he had to wait until his mother got home.

Here we all were on the beach the time the kids buried Shannon in sand up to his head, and there was Madam cantering on a chestnut mare through a green Irish field.

A note from John I found on the kitchen counter at the Cape one morning when he had let himself in by climbing through the laundry room window again. He just wanted me to know he'd come in late and would see me in the morning, and even that simple note, he signed with love.

There were the pictures of them all locked away in my memory as well, of all the everyday moments historians never recorded and cameras never captured since that day I became, no matter how hard I resisted, a part of this family.

Five years passed, then ten, then fifty.

Where were you when it happened, Kath?

The question echoed across the span of my lifetime, and I knew the answer I wished I could tell them all now, as I turned the last page before closing my book of memories.

With you, I would say.

I was always with you.

ACKNOWLEDGMENTS

When I sit back and think of all the people I would like to thank for making this dream a reality, I realize how fortunate I am to have so many amazing people in my life. Where do I even begin?

First, my parents. I want to thank my dad for sending me and my sister to America for a better life. As a mother and grandmother, I realize now how hard a decision that must have been. Which leads me to my mom. I know what a major sacrifice it was for her to let us leave and how much it broke her heart, and I want to thank her for allowing us to go.

I want also to thank my siblings—to the memory of my beloved baby sister, Mary, and my brother, Michael, and to my sister Briege and brothers Packy, John, Jim, and Owney—and all those back home in Inniskeen. My family is the world to me; I can't thank them enough for all they have done to shape the person I am today.

ACKNOWLEDGMENTS

A huge thank-you to my husband, Seamus, for all the hard work and support he has put into this project. His belief in me and in my story kept me going, as did the encouragement and help from my immediate family: Clare, Merrill, Keira, Conlin, and Braden McIntire; Shane, Laura, and Quinn McKeon; and Heather, Ryan, Eamon, and Ronan O'Dell.

Speaking of family, I want to thank Pat and Rose for taking us into their home and caring for us like family right alongside their own children.

To Bridget, Patricia, John, and Kathleen for their kindness and patience.

To Jack Maloney and Mugsy for getting me the interview with Jackie.

And to my dear friends at our beautiful beach in Rocky Point, which we call the Irish Riviera!

My friends on the tennis court at Verona Walk, and my close friends and neighbors in our little paradise, the Isles of Capri.

Family and friends are the true treasures in life, and I feel fortunate to have so many of them.

Finally, I want to thank all the creative geniuses behind the scenes:

Christina Cush for helping me with the book proposal and for finding my amazing agents, Jeff Kleinman and Steve Troha at Folio Literary Management. Finding them was like finding family! They got me on the right track. Also, many thanks to Jamie Chambliss at Folio, for working her magic on the proposal.

And Tamara Jones, for her wonderful writing and ability to weave my stories together. She has an amazing talent for which I am eternally grateful.

I also want to thank the amazing team at Gallery Books, Simon and Schuster. When I first met Jen Bergstrom, Mitchell Ivers, and Jen Robinson, I felt an instant connection. I knew I had found my publishing dream team. I'm also incredibly blessed to have the editorial support of Jackie Cantor. My deepest thanks also to Louise Burke, Liz Psaltis, Natasha Simons, Marla Daniels, Sarah Wright, Shelly Perron, Lisa Litwack, and Ella Laytham. From Mrs. Kennedy I learned the value of teamwork and what it means to have trusted people by your side. What an incredible and talented group you all are!

And finally, thank you, the reader, for taking the time to read the story of my life.